A LIFE FOR DANCE

RUDOLF LABAN

A LIFE
FOR
DANCE

Reminiscences

WITH DRAWINGS BY THE AUTHOR

Translated and annotated by Lisa Ullmann

MACDONALD & EVANS LTD.

8 JOHN STREET, LONDON WC1N 2HY

1975

First Published February 1975

©

MACDONALD AND EVANS LIMITED
1975

ISBN: 0 7121 1231 6

Printed in Great Britain by
J. W. Arrowsmith Ltd., Bristol BS3 2NT

TRANSLATOR'S PREFACE

WHEN in the English-speaking world so many people kept asking me what Laban was like as a man, how he arrived at his ideas, and to what kind of influences he was exposed, I finally decided to prepare a translation of his book *Ein Leben für den Tanz* which was published in Germany in 1935.

Here he himself gives answers to many of the questions, although the book embraces only the period of his life up to the early 1930s. In it Laban tells mainly of events, experiences, thoughts and actual developments and relates them to his inner vision of dance.

In following his account it may add a further dimension to the understanding of the man and his work if the reader can see it against the background of the time, places and prevailing cultural, social and scientific conditions to which it refers. Today, when so many of the seeds which were sown in the early decades of this century have already been harvested and brought into common use, it is difficult to imagine the beginnings.

Laban with his clear vision, revolutionary spirit and inner strength made important contributions toward the thoroughgoing renewal of dance. As the reader will no doubt sense, everything had the freshness and wonder of new discovery, of new learning. There was boundless enthusiasm for searching, experimenting and conquering—and a conviction that dance must become reunited with its roots, which lie in the centre of our being.

In this book we can follow Laban's imagination, artistic sensibility and creative intentions. He does not touch upon the systematic research and the development of his theories which went alongside. With this book Laban has, as it were, concluded a chapter and a particular side of his life which was fundamental in his development. In his later years—he came to England in 1938 and died there in 1958—he was able to consolidate further his knowledge and understanding of movement and dance, explain their intrinsic nature and inspire informed application in ever wider fields of human activity.

However, in all this Laban never abandoned his ultimate aim, that dance should give joy to people.

The actual translation of this book presented considerable difficulty as I wanted to give the English reader the feel of Laban's way of writing which is so bound up with his thinking. Fortunately, I had the collaboration of Patricia Woodall in tackling this task. With her help and sensitive empathy, I hope we have been able to render the text in a readable form, in spite of keeping as closely as possible to a literal translation. It is with sincere gratitude that I recognise Patricia Woodall's unstinted patience, indefatigable care and generosity with her time in reviewing the text over and over again.

At an earlier stage, several years ago, a draft translation was prepared by Helen Heaton. I wish to tender to her my very warmest appreciation and acknowledgment. Without her devoted work, it would not have been possible to bring out this book; on the one hand, it was essential for the publishers to have a preview of its content, and on the other it has served as a basis for the present translation.

Finally, I hope that my annotations will help the reader to trace the geography of the events, place them in time and identify some of the personalities involved without destroying for him the enjoyment of the lively interplay in the book of reality and fantasy.

To go further will be the work of a biographer.

LISA ULLMANN

Addlestone, Surrey
January, 1974

A LETTER FROM THE AUTHOR TO HIS PUBLISHER TAKING THE PLACE OF A FOREWORD

Dear Mr. Schumann,

I have had no peace since you asked me to comment on the content and aim of my new book, and find a suitable title for it. So I shall now try to enlarge on the few lines which I sent you recently and also give you a brief idea of the thread running through my story and of its background.

Fundamentally it is the simplest thing in the world. I recount in my book how a human being makes his way through thousands of circumstances and events. Since this person happens to be a dance master or even a dance-poet, the book will frequently speak about the precious little-known art of dance. The whole kaleidoscope of events, both gay and serious, revolves around dance dramas, plays and festivals which that dance master has invented. This is because he is so dedicated to his art that the most important milestones in his life are not his love affairs or business successes, but the achievements in his work. The book also suggests that there may be a certain connection between the general cultural development of the time and the succession of works through which our dance master's talents unfold. This results in a round of events and thoughts in which various threads are interwoven, not least the thread on which are strung the pearls that come from the hidden waters of man's inner life. Only dance has the power to replenish the often almost dried-up springs of these waters effectively. Thus, our dance master found an even more profound challenge in his Dance of Life.* Every task is a gift from unknown forces. It is these forces which drive each development to its turning-point, whether it be the development of our epoch, the development of the individual from happily enjoying himself to happily being at service; or the development of strength of character, which is mirrored in every event.

This brings me back to the beginning again. Someone else might find in the experiences of the dance master quite different threads and thoughts. Even if he is not looking for any, I hope he may be entertained for an hour or so by the dance master and his curious art without too much risk of becoming bored; for all life is enjoyable if one looks at it with enjoyment and pleasure. The dance master's *Dance of Life** has been along the path of joy. May all my work show the way to joy, even if it only rouses a brief smile in response to a few lines which have been read with pleasure.

Should we not call this book *The Path of Joy* or *On the Path to Joy?* Subtitle *A Dance of Life.**

With kind regards and best wishes for success in our collaboration,

Yours sincerely,
Rudolf von Laban

---

* In German *Lebensreigen*. See p. 4.

CONTENTS

LIST OF ILLUSTRATIONS

PART ONE

Chapter 1

THE FOOL'S MIRROR

THE *Fool's Mirror* was the most successful of my dance-plays—or at least the one I performed most often. For several winters I travelled up and down the length and breadth of various countries with it. But once when I was in Hollywood, that American film paradise, someone in the film business told me I was wasting my talents with personal appearances on the stage. "What you achieve in a year," he said, "we achieve in a day. Three hundred performances of your plays mean that three hundred thousand people have seen them. What does that add up to? It's not even the population of a small town. And you need at least a year if not more to get that far, whereas on a single evening we play to audiences of hundreds of thousands of people in various towns and at the same time. That's the way to become known. In the end nearly everybody from the Eskimo to the Australian bushman knows us—and it's also very profitable. Leave off doing these ridiculous mime-acts and make a film!"

Now, the art of dance is unfortunately—or thank heaven—an art which cannot be caught and canned by a machine. The dancer has only to do a big jump and he has given the camera the slip; or a few rapid whirls and the stupid screen will register a shapeless cloud. Dancing needs the whole, living person and plenty of space into which he can project his happiness or sadness. He must also be able to control the element of time, for breathtaking speed may alternate with an almost unending

3

stillness of reflection. For these reasons I have not let my
Fool's Mirror be filmed.

There seems to be no other answer but to wait until a
really good Dance-Theatre has been built for me and a
well-paid dance-group has been formed. Then I shall
gladly perform the *Fool's Mirror* over and over again until
all the film fans, from the Eskimo to the Australian
bushman, have seen it. Meanwhile apart from the lucky
three hundred thousand or so who have seen the play
there are another four hundred million people in the
world. So for the sake of these poor deprived ones I will
say just a little about my *Fool's Mirror*.[1]

Imagine that this play sets out to portray the world
through the eyes of the fool. It's not that the fool is really
so very different from ordinary people though sometimes he may be a little happier or sadder than they are.
But his high spirits or moods of desperate sadness are on
the one hand such a pleasing, and on the other such a
horrifying, sight for his fellow creatures that he quickly
gets the idea that he should make acting his career.

In the *Fool's Mirror* there were two *Reigen*[2] or, if you
prefer it, two acts, one of which could be called the dance
of life and the other the dance of death. Nothing is more
natural than that one dance is exuberantly lively and the
other deathly sad. This happens in real life, too, fortunately in agreeable alternation.

The fool could dance the whole affair by himself, but to
lighten his task and also to give the audience more variety
he chooses a few dancers to play opposite him. They all
have two faces[3] and we will call them "Pridehumility,"

[1] The original German title of this dance-ballad was *Narrenspiegel*. It was first
performed by the Kammertanzbühne Laban in Berlin in November 1926.

[2] *Reigen* is usually translated as "round dance" and plays a fundamental role
in the evolution of dance. The word *Reigen* can also be used in connection
with a person's cycle of life as in *Lebensreigen*, or a series of thoughts as in
Gedankenreigen, or a dance work consisting of several consecutive parts as in
Reigenwerk. The distinctive nature of *Reigen* is that there is an assemblage of
events, thoughts or people whose single units are linked and progress in a
certain order which unfolds around a central theme and along a coherent
line. In dance a *Reigen* tends to be non-representational and lacks the drama
of antagonistic tension.

[3] In the *Fool's Mirror* the costumes were specially designed to show the two
sides of each character.

"Joygrief" and "Lovehate," even though their names were different on the programme.

Pridehumility is a solemn gentleman: in the mourning ceremony he is the cruel-but-kind master-figure of death; in the comedy of life he casts down his eyes.

Joygrief is a woman who endures the dance of life and transmits forgiving compassion in the dance of death, even bringing radiance to grief.

Lovehate is also a woman who loves life and hates death.

There are a number of other people who, as clowns in the dance of life, enjoy themselves and find everything marvellous and who play dignified mourners in the dance of death.

But what is the play about?

My old friend Kasperl,[4] from the Kasperl Theatre of my childhood, once remarked:

"D'you know, people don't really like the theatre! All they like is gorging themselves with food and drinking themselves silly, and that's it."

Though I respected his wisdom I had to disagree with him, at least as far as it concerned tomfoolery. I could count on the fingers of one hand those fools who over-indulge in food and drink. But the other kind, the lovesick fools, you could almost ask who isn't one? I therefore chose love for the prime folly, because it contains everything: pride and humility, joy and grief, and not least, hate, the other side of love.

It is difficult to describe in words what my three dream-figures performed around me—for I danced the fool—because it was just a dance. But I can tell you how I came to create this strange play.

It all sprang from memories of the Kasperl theatre which I had played with as a child. Of course, it wasn't about love then, but about a magic blue flower.

The principal actors in my Kasperl Theatre, apart from Kasperl and the devil, were some peasantwomen,

[4] Kasperl is the German equivalent of Punch and the Kasperl Theatre is a Punch and Judy Show. Laban would have seen travelling Punch and Judy Shows and also, as is clear from the text that follows, had his own Kasperl Theatre at home, and made up his own dramatised stories.

an oarsman and an actor. My favourite play was symbolic in character. It dealt with a dark chapter of our family history. My father had several brothers, all of them in important, dignified and influential positions except one. This brother had not toed the line, but had gone on the stage and had become one of the most famous actors of his day in Germany. As soon as he entered the theatrical profession however, he was forbidden to use the family name.[5] With secret anxiety my family now began to detect certain similarities between myself and this prodigal son. To make matters worse, I also unfortunately resembled in looks and ways a legendary great-uncle who had seriously displeased his contemporaries through various extraordinary enterprises, such as founding a rowing club. As a warning, the strange end of this eccentric man was described to me in the most horrifying detail. Having spent the best days of his life on the great river,[6] he was found dead in a boat. I couldn't help sympathising with these two outcasts and together with Kasperl and the devil they became the heroes of my first play. But to explain the plot and particularly the role of the good peasant women, I must go further back in my story.

The house where I was born[7] looked out on to the same huge river on which my great-uncle had met his ignominious death. Opposite the windows through which my uncomprehending eyes had first looked out on to the splendours of the world stood the legendary boathouse which he had built. It was the only building in sight and was surrounded by ageless, silvery tree-giants stretching out in all directions along the riverbanks and deep into the countryside. There was also an old meadow where witches and goblins mingled with countless gnats. Twisted roots of trees had been laid bare by the waves of the huge river and the only sandy and sunny beach was

---

[5] This was Adolf Mylius, classical actor in Hamburg's City Theatre towards the end of last century and recognised as a great artist.

[6] The Danube.

[7] Laban was born on 15th December 1879 in Poszony in Hungary, now Bratislava in Czechoslovakia.

near the boathouse from which frisky little boats took off. These I could watch happily for hours on end. But there were other strange-looking vessels on the river, barges covered with gigantic roses in all colours. From these roses welled up a solemn chant accompanied by the gentle peal of bells. The gigantic roses were really the huge brightly-coloured skirts of peasantwomen who, as I learned later, had been on a pilgrimage to do penance. In my childish ignorance I used to call them the "Rowing Club,"[8] the same name I gave the people who flitted about in the little boats, although I couldn't pronounce the "R" then.

Our great-grandmother lived quite near us and we often used to visit her. In the quiet of the evenings she would tell us about a blue flower which bloomed on a great rock in the old meadow. Whoever picked this flower would become immortal. But nobody had ever been able to reach it and those who had tried had come hurtling down, stone-dead. She would tell us this and other stories when we were tired out from dancing all over the leather sofa and around the round table. By that time the old chiming clock above the sofa would sound almost melancholic, and we would sit down at her feet, tucked into her wide pleated skirt, and look up at her mild, kind face under its white bonnet. She would also tell us stories of the famous Emperor "Napoleum,"[9] who must have been a real rascal. When my grandfather was a little boy he used to crawl under the bed in terror when "Napoleum" and his rough troop of soldiers marched past our windows—the same windows by which great-grandmother was now sitting. That is how it came about that the devil in my Kasperl theatre was called "Napoleum."

"Who creeping round the bush has come,
I think it is Napoleum."

[8] The German for rowing club is *Ruder Club*. Laban "as a child" pronounced it *Luder Club* which means "Rascal Club."

[9] "Napoleum" was a slang form of Napoleon which was widely used because it rhymed with so many German words—*um, herum*, etc.

With this little rhyme Kasperl opened nearly all our
plays. Eventually the devil would appear and bring the
necessary commotion into the otherwise uneventful
story.

In my symbolic plays both heroes, the actor uncle and
the rowing club uncle, were under the protection of
Kasperl, and the peasantwomen in their colourful skirts
were angels of some kind. I was convinced of their piety
not only because of their pilgrimages but also because of
another event. Great-grandmother used to tell us that all
people, after they had died, would dance on God's own
green meadow, just as we did now around the table.
Once, when I was watching a wedding in a nearby village,
I saw peasantwomen dancing on the green in front of the
church. I was quite sure that they were dead and, because
they looked so lovely, that they must be angels. After that
I could not rest until I had at least three peasantwomen in
my theatre to complete my heavenly chorus and they too
came under the protection of Kasperl. Only the devil
"Napoleum" mostly appeared alone. He should really
have had an entourage of witches and goblins from the
old meadow, but the costumes and scenery gave me
enough headaches as it was and I decided to dispense
with the idea of a devil's chorus.

As soon as Kasperl had made his opening speech,
"Napoleum," with a diabolical laugh, would enter the
scene pushing a boat with dead great-uncle in it. Kasperl
would then confer with the actor uncle what to do next.
They decided to find the blue flower up on the dangerous rock so that they could revive great-uncle. After
untold difficulties, uncle succeeded in winning the blue
flower. "Napoleum" then got into a frightful rage and
resolved to steal the flower. He tricked poor uncle into
allowing him to sniff at it, snatched it away from him and
pushed him into the boat with dead great-uncle in it.
"Napoleum" had, of course, planned to abduct both
corpses to hell. At that moment, the pious peasantwomen
appeared on the scene and began their hallelujahs. This
was too much for the devil and he retreated at the sound
of these holy songs, losing his two souls and in the end

getting soundly spanked. As soon as he had departed to hell, everyone joined in a joyful dance, and the two resurrected heroes were highly feted and praised.

The reader will observe that my childhood play has a happy ending. Time has taught me to think differently. It is the devil more often than not who keeps the blue flower.

My next work, a melodrama, which I acted alone, had a far gloomier ending. Like most boys I had once run away from home to seek better people in better worlds—as a ship's apprentice, of course. My dramatic capture and the cruel treatment I suffered formed the text of my next ballad, *The Desolate Prisoner*, who, through the bars of his cell, naturally saw a star shining in the distance. Before escaping from my family I had smashed some of the windows at my school and had been expelled. My guardians managed to get me taken back conditionally, much to my regret, for I would far rather have gone away to learn a craft. So the ballad of the "desolate prisoner" became an outlet for my unhappiness and I recited it on every possible occasion. From then on I often found release from intense joy or grief by inventing and performing various kinds of ballads.

A lot of water had yet to flow down the great wide river by our family home before I composed the *Fool's Mirror*. Since then the river has been controlled and a stone embankment built, for all too often it burst its banks and flooded the countryside. During that time, Lovehate and Pridehumility were born in addition to Joygrief, and their actions and emotions are reflected in the *Fool's Mirror*. There was much laughter during these performances, but the audience was also deeply moved and we could feel it on the stage. It was one of our most vivid dance-works, otherwise not so many people would have come to see it. It also brought me the honour of being compared to Shakespeare. I am not recounting this out of vanity, but for the sake of dance-composers of the future to whom Shakespeare could indeed be an inspiration to create tragic-comic, comic-tragic dance-works which could open the eyes of the general public to the blessings of dance-experience.

I also want to mention here the event which gave me the idea of staging my ballads as *tableaux vivants*. It happened in a roundabout way because, as I have already recounted, my childhood guardians had little sympathy with my theatrical talents.

I sought comfort in painting, an art which was considered far more respectable than stage-craft because of Raphael and because it was generally preferred even by the Popes. All my leisure-hours were spent with my old friend, the painter.[10] He resembled Rembrandt with his twirled-up, bristly moustache, but there the resemblance ended. His artistic principle was strict adherence to nature, and sound technique in the use of the paintbrush. He regarded my self-taught daubings with contempt although I was already getting quite a reputation as a budding painter. He was the first person to whom I confessed my intention of becoming an artist, and from that day on he took me firmly in hand and forced me to learn real craftmanship, for which I am eternally grateful to him. He taught me both to observe and to perceive, and introduced me to his philosophy of life, the principles of which were love of work, scrupulous fulfilment of duty and unaffected behaviour. I respected him greatly for this. His countless sketches and pictures revealed more to me than I learned from all my school- or story-books. He would always maintain, however, that life depended on the builders and not on the genius, and that builders had to work with precision and diligence if their houses were not to collapse. If I dared to disagree, I was punished by having to mix paints and wash brushes all day long, and I loathed it. This training might sound pedantic but it was certainly of great educational value to me, especially if one takes into account my fertile imagination and carefree social background. It also brought about an unexpected development. Until then my pursuit of the arts had just been an

[10] See p. 167.

enjoyable pastime, a kind of escape from boring everyday duties and imposed disciplines, for such was the
extent to which I had been poisoned by my environment.
Through the influence of this excellent man my pastime
soon turned into a serious duty and I learned to recognise the value and significance of work. Where my other
tutors had failed this old man succeeded with his loyalty
to his craft. I was gifted with sensibility for the visual and
plastic arts and there was no other way to my inner self, to
my character, than through a craft that corresponded to
my talents. Awareness of movement existed only in my
sub-conscious and was strongly linked with the pictorial.

It needed a special occasion to open my eyes to the fact
that in the "moving picture" lies hidden a tremendously
enhanced expression of human will and feeling. My
master was often called upon to decorate halls for various
festivities and to invent and produce all sorts of embel-
lishments and surprises. I became his factotum and
assistant, at first in a rather menial role, when I was only
allowed to do the odd jobs, to lug things about, knock
them up and glue them together. Later on I was occasionally allowed to help in planning or even in submitting
designs.

Then came a memorable day when I discovered *tableaux vivants.*[11] The provincial ruler was coming for the
unveiling of a great monument. We were asked not only
to design triumphal arches but also *tableaux vivants* which
were to be put on at the city theatre.[12] My pride knew no
bounds when I was allowed to get my fancifully-dressed
friends and relatives into the oddest positions. With one
group, which was to be formed round the bust of the
ruler I had tried out all sorts of positions while my master
was away and when he returned I showed them to him
one after the other. When I gave the word "Now, ladies
and gentlemen, position number one!" the pianist struck
up a flourish. And so on for number two and all the rest.
My master and the corporation who were also there

[11] Laban was then approximately sixteen years of age and still a schoolboy.
[12] In Bratislava.

FIG. 1.—The fool and Death.

found each new tableau more enchanting than the last, so finally it was decided to show all of them as a sequence, each one with an increasingly dramatic musical flourish. That was how my first moving *tableau vivant* was created, and it opened up a completely new field of activity to my imagination. No more cleaning brushes and suchlike. I designed hundreds of these sequences and gradually they developed into real group-dance scenes.

Chapter 2

THE EARTH

AMONG my early sketches I found drafts for a large-scale
Reigenwerk with song, which I had called *The Earth*. They
showed streams of red, green and blueish-white colours
which represented groups of people. The red ones were
the souls of animals, the green the spirits of plants and
the blueish-white ones the spectres of crystals.

In my childhood the earth was my confidante. She was
the mistress of giants and elves, woodsprites and water-
nymphs. Over and over again one had to flee the
forest—because it was alive with spirits and demons and
they were everywhere in thousands of shapes and forms.
Or was the dragon crawling through the mist in the old
meadow and the dance of the will-o'-the-wisps, which
even other people could see above the bog, just
imagination? Weren't there witches careering about in
the tangled willows and goblins and gnomes skipping at
sunset between the red-glowing tree trunks? Surely I
couldn't be mistaken even if they did change so suddenly
into stilt-legged birds or scurrying squirrels. And hadn't
those sparkling stones at the entrance to the cave down in
the inhospitable valley come from the treasury of the
mountain-king? Wasn't that a nymph's hand reaching
out to the fishes leaping playfully in the river? And wasn't
there a beautiful white figure quite clearly visible beneath
the great wave, weaving and swaying in a fantastic
dance?

Mountains are giants. Now as then I can feel how I climb along the flank of one.[1] I scramble up his ragged chest, clutching at each hair to pull myself up. Stones fall behind me, the sun beats down, but at last I reach the top. The giant has a single eye in his forehead. When I take off my clothes and put them in the sun to dry the gusty wind whirls my shirt and trousers up into the air, and straight down into the eye where they float about. It is a mountain tarn so deep that it is bottomless, the edges green, the centre black; an eye without eyelashes, the eye of a bald giant. On top of his pointed head he wears a white snowcap even in the middle of summer. There is nothing for it but to plunge into that cold tarn and retrieve my garments. I hear mocking laughter behind me, or are my ears buzzing? Isn't that a little imp or gnome sneaking up to watch a small naked boy fishing his clothes out of the giant's eye? The inquisitive imp slips under a stone and now he looks like a lizard. I look for the vanished imp in vain, then carefully tuck my precious belongings underneath the stone, climb on to a hump of rock—maybe it's the giant's nose—and look down into the eye. Above me is a clear, cloudless sky and below the inhospitable wrinkles and warts of the giant's skin. I stretch out my arms towards the sun and take a deep breath. Now a shiver runs across my back and I look again into the open eye of the drowsing giant. Insolently he cocks it at the sky. Why do the gods allow such monstrous laziness? Laziness is said to be a sin! Can't one rouse this rascal into a puffing and a trembling as the last earthquake did, and that wasn't long ago considering the length of his life? Then at least he would turn over on to his other huge flank or burrow deep down into the earth, his giant-mother.

Did I—the gnat on the giant's nose—stand there for many thousands of years or only for a fleeting moment? However long it was, so many and such momentous things happened at that time.

[1] Laban refers here to the Tatra mountains where as a child he frequently spent his holidays.

I could see it all: the giant stretching, tossing and turning, then settling down, slowly arranging the folds of his skin and tensing all his humps. Now he lies back deceptively, looking as if he is going to stay like that for ever. Then suddenly and alarmingly, he stirs. Everything dies, is suffocated, and crushed. Steam and dust, floods and sparks shoot from nowhere. He rears and then lazily falls back again and lies barren in the sun. Such is the life of giants.

Does he feel the same shiver passing through him as we humans do when we are frightened or when we take a deep breath because we feel happy and healthy?

A dark red-rimmed wall of clouds gathers on the horizon. It devours the sky. When the sky is gone silence falls and people are gloomy, but when it smiles we understand it, laugh with it and feel happy. As it gets darker, the giants hold their breath. Wild, dark rags of clouds creep over the mountain precipices. Suddenly, a fiery spear, a flash of lightning, hurtles through the air towards the giant's head. He ducks. A tremendous crash rends the air in the valleys. The giants roar and thunder in answer. Huge hailstones and a raging wind nearly knock me to the ground.

When as a child I roamed about in the mountains, woods and meadows I always felt as if I received answers to questions which I could ask nobody but the earth. This time even heaven spoke to me. Heaven and earth are father and mother of man, I thought, and I rejoiced to be a human being and jubilantly raced the rapid brooks down into the valley.

All this I experienced as a child and I shall never forget it.

I remember a room in my grandparents' house which became decisively important later in my life. It was a large oval-shaped music room with golden wallpaper and white doors and standing in a niche there was a life-sized marble figure of a youth holding a lyre. I was free to use this room as I liked. I began to try out various familiar tunes on the grand-piano until at last melodies of my own came to me. The golden room became the scene of strange dreams. The marble-god was to me the most noble image of an earthly creature and I often felt as if the lyre emitted soft sounds and that my melodies came from it to me.

One day it became a roar, reminding me of my adventure near the giant's eye. I saw a solemn throng of children of the earth, transparent, luminous human souls. They called beseechingly to the demon of heaven. They tried to rise higher and higher, nearer to him, into the clouds. But the giants on earth seized them and they crashed down in terrible confusion into the deep valleys.

The earth groans and the spirits break into a chant:

"Demon, Demon, create thy creature!"

Then the song of the demon rings out. He creates the soul of the animal.

Yet the song of the animal eluded me. I imagined it should be wild and strong and gigantic, but the marble-god behind me had become silent.

Some time later I went to spend the holidays with my parents. The train passed through a long tunnel and back into the light. The sea![2] For the first time in my life I saw the blue infinity. There were a few white sailing-boats on it, some of them swaying lightly, others gliding quietly. Soon, however, I was going to come to know the sea in quite a different way.

It was midnight when we boarded the ship. I slept soundly through the night and only seemed to dream that I was either standing on my head or rolling down a slope. In the morning I found getting dressed a very amusing performance as I kept being thrown from one end of the cabin to the other. Then when I came up on deck I saw before me a green wall of water. It sank and immediately rose again, while all round me were mountains of water on which our comparatively small ship rolled perilously. The hellish noise, a mixture of howling

[2] The Adriatic. Laban, a boy of approximately twelve years, was on his journey to the Balkans where his father was stationed. The following descriptions are of experiences which he had on various visits during the next few years.

winds and roaring waters, was broken by sirens hooting
at short intervals. The moaning and groaning of the ship
sounded almost piteous. Not a soul was to be seen. I clung
to a rail and stared at the green darkness. Where were my
friendly nymphs and gnomes, my elves and giants whom
nature had taught me to trust? Here was only one thing:
a huge sinister snake. But was it underneath us, or had it
already swallowed us up and were we even now rolling
about in its glassy bowls? Where was the sky? Where the
earth? Sea-spray and clouds of mist enclosed us. I clung
to the rail like a wet fly. The green wall slanted one way
and then another; sometimes it was above me and then
again beneath. Now it disappeared altogether just as
trees do when we whirl past them on a merry-go-round.
Later I learnt from the captain that we had passed
through a strait which was always a bit choppy. Meanwhile, all the ship's rooms had been searched for me, as it
had seemed quite inconceivable that anybody would go
on deck in such heavy seas. What bliss it had been to get
up so early with nobody there to stop me! My acquaintance with the mighty snake had been wholly to my
liking. The earth was the mother of giants, I concluded,
the sea the mother of the snake.

It was many years later when I sailed again,[3] for eight
days and nights, between mountains of water in a storm
far worse than the one before, but I could never get
enough of this wonderful sight. The sea is an unpredict-
able creature. When it is smooth and calm, when the
great silvery plate is perfectly still and stretched out from
horizon to horizon, it is beyond imagination that it could
rise again, rear up and strike fear into people's hearts.
Dolphins at play, fast-hurtling sharks, an occasional
whale with its modest fountain, the smoke of a far-off
steamer—they are all as nothing, mere specks of dust on
the snake-like demon's great mirror. The phosphores-
cent frolicking of the sea, the shafts of sunlight and the
moonbeams curling on the water do not belong to the
snake. Glittering, deceitful and indifferent, he lets the

[3] In 1926 he visited the United States, sailing on a slow boat.

ripples play and glisten over his skin. His quietness is
soothing. Yet he lives, he pounces, he rebels, he domi-
nates, he threatens. He is a dragon whom one can resist
but not conquer; a power greater than all the powers, the
mightiest demon of the earth; the perpetually lurching,
heaving, surging sea.

A naked, barren mountain greeted us on arrival:
nothing but stones right down to the sea, with the town
on the shore like a heap of gravel, grey as the mountain.
There were mountains with unruly hair and soft, velvety,
black jungle-forests in the trackless valleys. It was a land
of animals, plants and rocks, a land of adventure![4]

We rode over the desolate, sun-scorched plain. We
covered many miles, our goal a poplar near the minaret
of a mosque. The two spires stood together in the clear
sky, one deep-black the other snow-white. We tore along
across country on our small, swift horses. There were no
tracks. Crevasses, landslides, and dried-up riverbeds
appeared out of nowhere and had to be scrambled over.
Snakes, adders, sandvipers dangled from low branches
and basked in the sun. We passed the dark, secluded lake
of Jezero, surrounded by impenetrable jungle. An eagle
circled high over the waters, higher than the naked, red
wall of rock which towered above the jungle. Chamois
skipped along looking very tiny in the distance. An eagle
swooped down like a black god, snatched up one of the
little creatures and carried it away, far over the glowing
rock. Then he disappeared into the yellow sky.

In winter hunger drove the wolves to our camp. A
boathouse, built on stilts, stood near the lake where we
would skate, and a rickety staircase led down to the
frozen water. On the opposite bank was the slaughter-
square, where the frozen blood of the slaughtered
animals formed a fantastic, bumpy ice-landscape of red
and yellow marble. It is all present in me still: the wolves

[4] Laban's father was a high-ranking officer in the Austro-Hungarian empire
and military governor of Bosnia and Herzegovina. He was stationed at the
fort of Nevesinje near Mostar where Laban frequently went and found the
"land of adventure." The population was mainly Moslem and the country
extremely wild and primitive.

are drawn to it although the blood is frozen. I skate along over the mottled bumps, an ice-sail in my hand. A few soldiers wave to me from the boathouse. They call out but their words are lost in the wind. I look round. A dozen dots appear from nowhere at full speed—wolves! My sail against the wind is only a hindrance. I throw it away and begin to skate for my life. But the brutes come closer and closer. At last I reach the rickety staircase. I slip on the ice-covered steps and my skates get stuck. With a last burst of energy I pull myself free and leap into the boathouse. I collapse on my knees, in front of the big glass window that looks on to the lake and stare into the blood-red throats of the wolves. In famished fury they jump up to the window, their claws screeching on the glass. One pane breaks.

We have six bullets in our pistol. Three shots kill two wolves but the other bullets we have to save, because the whole of the boathouse-wall cracks and shakes from the onslaught of the furious animals. The surviving wolves fall upon their dead mates, tear them to pieces and devour them, leaving hardly a bone or bloodstain. Then they are off over the frozen lake into the distance.

An adventure near the snake mountain was also not exactly a joke and it was an excellent lesson for later life. Some hundreds of metres high rose a snow-white cone, its south, east and west sides nothing but scree without a branch of a tree or a blade of grass on them. Having just arrived, we two boys, a new-found friend and I, had no inkling of the treachery of this mountain. It was as round as a ball and wonderfully smooth—very inviting for romping about. The north side was easier for climbing up as it was not so steep and was also wooded in places, and once on top we could whizz down the steep southern slope. But the descent did not go as well as we had hoped. There was no firm foothold, so we had to squat. The stony surface consisted of pebbles and at a touch they began to roll down. We found we could sit quite comfortably in this gently-moving pebble-stream and let it carry us down to the valley, and we sensed no danger. But who can describe our horror when snakes kept emerging from behind every third or fourth stone. Soon scores of green and brown spirals accompanied us on our down-hill-slide and we recognised them distinctly as poisonous snakes. But there was no stopping, no return; only a ghastly struggle to avoid the ubiquitous snakes. Hadn't we seen a Turk passing our garden the other day? Half an hour later they carried his body away—his face blue and swollen. He had drunk some milk out in the field and then lain down for a moment. A few drops had stayed on his beard. A snake came to lap them up. The sleepy peasant felt a touch and tried to brush it away. At that the snake bit into his lip and a few minutes later his comrades found him dead. These memories and other snake-tales darted through our minds as we tried to avoid these neat little spirals as much as possible. A moss-covered boulder checked the shute of stones. We leapt on to this island of escape and the hissing snakes scattered around us. When we got home and said we had been on the white moun-tain there was a terrific commotion. We were told that it was called the snake mountain and that no sensible person had set foot on it for generations.

One morning I saddled my horse and went off all by myself. A delightful ride took me to a stony wilderness, high in the mountains! Boulders of rock stood there like small houses, a whole city, a sea of grotesque shapes. They were big enough to hide rider and horse. The wilderness drew me further and further on with no idea of time and not a care in the world. I completely forgot to look where I was going. Two sinister-looking Turks were lying propped against a stone. I dismounted to rest my horse, for the long ride over the rough stony track had tired him considerably. I was just about to ask these two ragged ruffians the best way home, for I felt as if I had been riding round in a circle and one rock looked just like another. Suddenly, I felt suspicious of them. Then another man appeared from behind me, peered over a rock and called out to the other two. They made for my horse which reared up high. I jerked it round, flung myself into the saddle and turning sharply at the rock saw a downhill stretch on which I could gallop at least for a time. The three toughs, cursing and armed with knives, tried to overtake me with long leaps, or rather to cut off my escape. But my horse sped like the wind and bolted at a breathtaking pace. Between stones, over stones, like a gazelle—magnificent how these small mountain horses can go so swiftly. They are pure-bred arabs with nothing of the mule or other cross-breed about them; courageous and intelligent and the most loveable animals I have ever met. It was the cunning and swiftness of my "Ali" that had saved me, because I was told at home that I had strayed onto a notorious plateau, unsafe since the war-time occupation. Nobody was ever supposed to go there unarmed or alone, and even visitors who went in two's or three's often returned minus ears or noses, parts of the body that were as desirable trophies there as scalps were for the Red Indians.

Now I could complete the song of the animal. Now I knew how both courage and greed towered in its soul like an unyielding rock; how its death-pounce was like lightning and its roar like a howling storm.

Back in the golden music-room I went on dreaming: my songs of the earth were not yet ready. In my movement-sketches I showed the green plants and the blue crystals, and now phantasy enriched these movement images with new happenings. The giants set snares to tame the fury of the animals. The spirits call for the demon. He sees the fettered, dying animal and breathes a new soul into it, the soul of the plant.

Again, it was the land of adventure which opened up my understanding of the plant with its profuse growth and its bewitching scent. Again in that land there flowed in on my senses the song of the choir of spirits which was to praise the new wonder of the earth in a beguiling elegiac chant.

The deep gorges of the land of adventure were overgrown with impenetrable jungle. It was possible to get close to them, and lured by giant raspberries we even dared to go further in, if only a short distance. There were rumours that the wolves, bears and wild boars, which came close to our camp in winter, retreated during the hot summer months into the thickets of these jungles, and multitudes of the inevitable snakes were also said to live there. After our earlier experiences we now decided on caution and kept near to the outskirts of the forest, all the more because it was almost impossible to penetrate further.

It is difficult to describe these gorges and the impression they make. There are no tracks, no paths. Narrow vertical cuttings, the width of a stream, wind their way for many miles and lead to broader valleys, overgrown with forest. One shivers in these gorges and the musty air takes one's breath away. Everything looks black, even the crystal-clear water in the streams against the dark background. Hardly a plant is to be seen except for huge fantastic outcrops of moss. Rocks and screes obstruct the flow of the water and sometimes form magnificent arches above it. It is like wandering about in the subterranean vaults of a giant's castle. Suddenly, the cutting widens, but it gets no lighter because everywhere the thickly-matted plants cast a deep shade over the water. Branches of huge trees twist into one another; parasitic plants coil luxuriantly around them. The musty air takes on a sickly, sweet flavour. Complete silence reigns. Not a bird, not an animal stirs; here and there the stillness is broken by a soft rustling and humming which emanates from the tangled blackness. Here live the plants, plants by themselves, for themselves, greedy and self-indulgent. Whoever approaches is lulled to sleep by a gentle compelling power of the kind one experiences only in dreams. Earth, how terrible are your children!

I conceived the song of the plant—the mighty, in-drawing, craving thirst of its soul—soon after my return from this dark Hades. Then the land of adventure inspired me to yet a third song, the song of the resounding hard stone, the glittering crystal, which the demon created when he petrified every living thing.

In rock fissures and deep caves, in magnificent dome-like grottos and mountain-caverns, alive with fantastic stalagmites and sparkling crystals, I experienced the meaning of the self-willed soul of the mineral.

We had found out that a great hoard of munitions was supposed to be hidden in one of the narrow, deep mountain-clefts. When we had reached the spot indicated and cleared the tangled undergrowth away, we stood in front of a crevasse measuring about ten metres long with a gap of about one and a half metres at its widest part. First we threw stones down and heard them falling endlessly. There were so many echoes that we could not be sure amid all the faint tinkles and reverberations when the stone had reached the bottom. Otherwise, we could have calculated the approximate depth of the crevasse from the moment of impact. Then we lowered some lanterns on ropes and saw that the walls of the crevasse went straight down with only slight projections. Even fifty-metre ropes did not touch the bottom however, and the lanterns went out, probably because of strong currents of air at that depth. It was then decided that some of us should go down. At first they wouldn't take me, but I insisted, and it was decided that I should go down third, after the first two had found a foothold. The first man had a field-telephone on him. At a depth of fifty metres, he reported that there were large passages branching off the main pothole and a platform on which twelve people could comfortably find room. The second man and I, as the third, were then lowered on ropes into the cold and humid narrow passage. When the three of us met, we took off our ropes, and tied them up securely so that we could move freely.

The vertical hole went down deeper, but even from this depth it was an unfathomable abyss, apparently getting narrower and narrower. At any rate, an examination with our lantern showed that after another thirty metres down there would hardly be room for a person to squeeze through. We were able to move quite comfortably along one of the side passages however, and after about a hundred steps we reached a vaulted dome big enough to contain a smallish house. Except for minute stalactites the walls were nearly smooth and almost formed a hemisphere, with rocks slightly overhanging the lower edge. We found no traces of munitions or people. Then one of my companions discovered a small round opening into which he unsuccessfully tried to force himself. Being the smallest and the shortest I could just about get through so they fastened a rope round me and after I had squeezed through they passed me my lantern. Suddenly, in the flickering light, I saw a white figure before me which gave me a fright. As I approached it I realised it was a stalagmite, rising from the ground. Soon I noticed one after another of these weird shapes around me as well as hundreds of thin spikes hanging from the low ceiling. It was like being caught between the teeth inside the mouth of a giant animal. The uneven ground sloped steeply and several times I fell down. Moreover, the rope to which I was fastened made it uncomfortable to advance in this narrowing forest of stone pillars and forced me, much to my regret, to turn back. I stayed for a little while, leaning against one of the yellowish-white apparitions, and let the light of the lantern play through the vault. The coming to life of these motionless spectres was an unforgettable sight, their glistening shapes and shadows presenting a movement-display so different from that of leaping animals or undulating forests. I was sure in my mind that the stone was alive and possessed a will of its own in its tenacious, slow crystallisation, and its fight against destruction by sun or water. I valued the experience more than the weapons which we did not find and which were the first things my companions asked me about when they had pulled me back through the narrow opening. I couldn't say much when we reached the top again, and the leader of our expedition decided that the best thing to do would be to widen the opening and send a level-headed adult into the innermost grotto.

When I saw how quicksand engulfs and buries plants, and how it devours them, or how vegetation tries to bind and conquer sand in untiring battle, I could feel something near to hatred arising from the small sand-crystals against the proliferation of plants and, in reverse, feel the desire and will of plants to spread over every stone, and wall. Yet, mountains, rocks and minerals are the primeval giants, while plants are nothing but a parasitical, superficial covering of the surface, and animals and humans are rare dwarfs in this desert, in this sea, on the colossal block of mother earth.

The third song was to the

> "Resounding crystal,
> Icy life of stone"

which became for me the symbol of the discerning, ingenious spirit of nature, as the plant became the symbol of the impulses of the life of feeling, of all the stirrings of the emotions. The animal, however, is the strongest archetype of that tremendous will and dynamic force which fills the whole of nature.

Yet the spirits of the earth are not satisfied with these forms. They call for fulfilment of the creator's will. Man is the last to appear at the demon's command. Animal, plant and stone are fused in man's nature into one single force, that so far bears no name. Man is the promise of the earth if he has the strength to unite the three elemental forces and bring them to the highest point of development.

It took me many years to complete this work in all its component parts. Then it soon became also possible to produce single scenes of *The Earth*. The most difficult task was finding suitable artists who came nearest to my vision of presentation. At last the time came when we could meet for rehearsals, and we managed to get a few scenes going.[5] Our performances were greeted with great enthusiasm by some people and with violent disapproval by others. On the whole, I must confess that the novelty of the subject and the mode of presentation was mostly rejected as being an artist's joke. I was not greatly

[5] Laban's first conception of *The Earth* dates back to 1897, but it was not until 1914 in Switzerland that several scenes from it were performed, *e.g. Die Grünen* (The Green Ones) with musical interludes also composed by him, and based on a scale of his own fashioning in which each tone is of equal importance. He notated it without bars and in a harmonic way. Suzanne Perrottet was the musical interpreter and Maja Lederer the singer. The latter was Laban's second wife, whom he had married in 1910. There were five children from this marriage.

concerned about the applause or rejection but was glad that the performances had given me an opportunity to clarify my ideas of presentation. In fact, where I had intended to use large choirs, I had to make do with a limited number of participants and one woman to sing the songs. With my small group I tried to conjure up on the stage through the medium of the moving human body the beauty and wildness of nature. Man cannot really equal the flexible leap of an animal; also the plant's secretive swaying and its striving towards the sun may well live in our hearts but it is not easy to perform. The crystal-clear shapes which are created by our limbs in space and which we see traced, for instance, by the measured movements of an attentive figure, have a quality of real reverence about them and demand a high degree of dedication.

The audience as a whole had little appreciation of these things as yet, and since our movements were performed in complete silence, without musical accompaniment, some of our spectators and critics thought we were making fun of them. Only a few people realised how very seriously I took my art. The indignation of experts, whose well-beaten tracks I purposely avoided, naturally contributed to the rejection, which even became aggressive at times. To judge by the ingenious selection of objects which were chosen to bombard us now and then it was obvious that the ammunition had been carefully brought from home beforehand. Where else could have been found, in moments of feverish excitement, all the many eggs, over ripe plums, potatoes and pieces of wood with which thanks for our achievements were expressed?

When we could not resist sending the missiles back, friends became foes and when, in the heat of battle, we happened to hit the nose of a sympathetically applauding spectator another of our rare wellwishers was lost. Simple and unsophisticated people were, however, always delighted with our performances. One young workman, deeply moved by the scenes of *The Earth*, wrote me one of the most wonderful letters I was ever to receive. Another time, an old sculptor left the hall sobbing. At first I thought that it was our art that had made him feel ill, but soon afterwards he came to see me and declared that for the first time in his life he had shed tears over a stage performance. Nothing ever meant so much to me as this letter and the tears of the old man—not even the many messages of thanks from royalties and prominent personages, the appreciations of experts, and the praises from converted enemies with which I have since been showered.[6]

However, we were far from wanting to chase wild dream-ideals in heroic resignation. We had neither the time nor inclination for such things. The life that pulsated through our work and which had to be grasped afresh every minute, kept up our courage to carry on, as did the fact that some people, usually the very ordinary ones, understood us. I have to admit that I had no talent

---

[6] After Laban's death in 1958 the organisers of the Modern Dance Holiday Courses in England arranged an opportunity for people to share in commemorating his spirit and ideals. During the Summer Course of August 1959 at Eastbourne, *The Earth* was created and performed (with over a hundred participants including many visitors from overseas) to a large audience of friends and associates. Sylvia Bodmer, Diana Jordan and Lisa Ullmann composed and produced this *Reigenwerk*, inspired by Laban's early descriptions and sketches, and interpreting them freely according to their own conception of the theme. There were three parts and the programme included poetry and choir singing as well as original music compositions by Adda Heynssen. It ran as follows:

1. Introduction to first part—words from the *Universe* by Rabindranath Tagore.
2. The Dance of Awakening—percussion.
3. The Dance of the Animal—music from *The Rite of Spring*: Stravinsky.
4. The Chorus: Lament—The Transformation—poem *Vegetation* by Kathleen Raine.
5. The Dance of the Plant—music Adda Heynssen.
6. Introduction to second part—The Mummers—words and mime.
7. The Voyage—music *The Storm* from Peter Grimes: Benjamin Britten.
8. The Pirates—music: Khachaturian.
9. Automation—music from the *Peacock suite*: Kodály and *Music Concrete*.
10. Introduction to third part—The Choir—music: Adda Heynssen; poem *The Sphere* by Kathleen Raine.
 The Chorus: Rejoicing.
11. The Dance of the Crystal—music: Adda Heynssen.
12. The Dance of Man—music: Adda Heynssen.

FIG. 2.—The birth of the animal.

whatsoever for fabricating easy-sellable products for the
theatre, a fact I often regretted in weak moments,
particularly in view of the financial needs of my helpers.
In years to come, however, the same selection of scenes
from *The Earth* were wildly and unanimously acclaimed
by audiences and the press. But it took years to educate
people in looking and discerning. It is not at all easy to
follow the movements of a dancer with one's eyes, and
what one cannot see one obviously cannot really judge.

Chapter 3

THE NIGHT

THE greatest failure of my life in the eyes of the press and
public was *The Night*. I thought it was an excellent piece
of work though it was only performed twice. It was
beautifully presented, cost ten times as much in money,
toil and heartache as the *Fool's Mirror* and had a cast of
ten times as many people. But obviously it is not quantity
that counts! I had originally given it the name of the
Queen of the Night. It represented in dance form a series
of events which I will now relate.

As a small boy the very first time that I stumbled
behind my uncle[1] over the threshold of the stage-door of
our town theatre I chanced to see the "Queen of the
Night," who was just asking the porter for her mail.

She was a majestic, fascinating sight, an imposing
woman with black hair, big, heavily outlined eyes and
long eye-lashes almost like a toothbrush—her face
strangely painted, her beautifully-shaped lips appearing
almost black. In those days one never saw a woman
wearing make-up outside the theatre. From her shoulders fell a long, black velvet coat, covered with silvery
stars. The Queen spoke a few friendly words to me in the
melodious voice of an actress. But when she bent down to
me with her glittering tiara, and lifted my chin, I was
suddenly frightened by the coarsely painted face so close

[1] He was Laban's uncle Antoine Sendlein, the husband of his father's sister
Anna. (*See also* p. 166.)

to my own, and I darted away through the door out into the theatre grounds and sat on a garden seat. The first stars began to appear in the sky. I looked across the illuminated windows of the theatre building to the realm of the "Queen of the Night."

Many years later, in the evening of the day when I had learnt that my wish to become an artist was to be fulfilled, I stood once again on the threshold of a stage door.[2] I had made friends with several actors and actresses and I now wanted to say good-bye to them. I gave the porter a message and waited in the courtyard outside the stage entrance for an answer. It was an ancient, dark court-yard, and the strange outlines of its sombre walls seemed to merge into the black shreds of clouds which were driving along the sky like smoke from a smouldering fire. The waxing moon was already quite bright. It looked ghostly behind the hurrying clouds and its light glanced over the cobble-stones of the courtyard. One of the patches of light seemed to leave the ground and come towards me. It was a woman in a moonlight-coloured dress, a dark shawl carelessly draped over her shoulders. She was one of the opera singers who had come herself to bring my friends' answer to my invitation to a farewell-party. By this time I had got used to theatrical make-up with its toothbrush eyelashes and all the trimmings. But here in the open, on this moonlight night, a great feeling of compassion came over me for the wretchedness of this ghostly pretence. The stage of the future—for me already a dethroned queen of the night—had to be something quite different. It must be a healthy festival of joy in the clear sunlight of day-time, without these pretences and trappings which smother all the essentials.

After the performance my friends and I left the theatre and drove out into the country to an inn on a hill. From its garden terrace the city below was a sea of lights. Soon, a long way from here in another, larger, city, I was to seek the realisation of my dreams. For a moment, in this happy-nostalgic farewell atmosphere, I felt a shadow of foreboding as if beneath the brilliant, glittering cloak

[2] This was in Vienna.

of the lighted streets and buildings there was an enormous monster that could crush all high hopes and expecta-
tions with one blow of his paw. Was the city just another
"Queen of the Night"?

All I took with me from my present life[3] was a number
of letters of introduction, among them one addressed to
a well-known, fashionable poet who was also a distant
relative. Other celebrities of the arts and society who I
called on with my letters politely evaded my requests for
advice on how to make my way, and only the fashionable
poet showed any interest. "I shall introduce you to
Madame X. She is a very competent woman with a lot of
connections in the theatre world; through her you will
meet the most famous men in the world."

There sat a woman, beautiful as a goddess, wearing an
incredible hat and loaded with sparkling jewellery—as
was the fashion in those days. She was seated as if on a
throne, slightly raised above a circle of elegant men of all
ages. "Queen of the Night" flashed through my mind
quite involuntarily, because she reminded me a little,
though she didn't wear a star-spangled cloak, of my
earliest theatre enchantress. She stretched out her hand
to me. Her long slender arm was fashionably covered
with dark gloves reaching above the elbow and I could
not help comparing her with my old friends in the land of
adventure, the graceful, beautiful vipers—banal as this
may sound. The men surrounding her competed in
saying or doing something exceptional. They obviously
wanted to draw the exclusive attention of the Queen of
the Night to themselves. One of them would stare into
a corner with exemplary stupidity; another would
automatically adopt a new pose every half
minute—movement habits in those days were quite
different from the ones to-day, a third would utter
nothing but short unfinished sentences, substituting an
elegant gesture of the hand for the unspoken ending;
and the fourth—my fashionable poet—chattered on and
on although nobody was listening. I sat there like the fifth
wheel of the triumphal coach of the goddess and felt

[3] Munich was the first port of call before Paris.

most uncomfortable. She looked out above our heads and smiled vaguely at the various groups of people who were stirring their teacups with an air of profundity, their little fingers affectedly crooked. Afterwards I felt as if nobody had spoken a single word of sense during the whole three-quarters of an hour of our visit. During this time I was also introduced to a number of people of both sexes, all politely grinning, but my fashionable poet took my arm and indicated that it was time to leave. I was given a slender viper-hand for a good-bye.

Social life didn't necessarily spoil people in those days, and nor does it today, but this last experience seemed to me the absolute peak of useless pretence and I swore to myself never to go there again. It did, however, give me an idea for a movement play satirising the meaningless gestures of the drawing-room.

Soon afterwards I received an invitation from the goddess to join her box at the opera. I didn't want to appear rude so I went and sat through the first act behind the cloud of chiffon in which she was swathed. During the interval she enquired attentively about how I was getting on in this big city, and, much to my surprise, seemed very well informed about my plans. "I believe you have a new kind of theatrical entertainment or something like that in mind. It interests me enormously. Do tell me about it." I told her that it was quite impossible to explain my plans and ideas in a few words during an opera interval and so we arranged to meet the following day and I promised to bring some of my sketches and notes.

The Queen of the Night turned out to be the first person to understand my art. I was delighted to have found a sympathetic soul. We talked of my dilemma in choosing a profession. "Didn't you have anyone to advise you"? she asked. I told her of an evening when I had discussed my future and my vocation with my grand-parents.

Our vineyards were situated outside the city[4] on a peaceful, sunny hillside and there on an unforgettable

[4] Bratislava.

autumn evening our conversation took place. In the
centre of the vineyards was an orchard in the shape of a
rectangle which stretched all the way up the hill. It was
surrounded by tall, old trees and thick bushes. Steps led
the whole length of the garden and up to a seat inside a
pergola. All along the steps were espaliers gleaming with
fruit. From the bottom I could see my grandparents
sitting on the seat high above me. Grandfather, with his
snow-white hair and his shining blue eyes, was to me the
essence of infinite kindness and complete understanding. Grandmother looked almost youthful at his side with
her graceful vitality. The bells of a small chapel in the
nearby village tolled for evensong. At the first peal of
bells I saw these two venerated people clasp each other's
hands. Attracted by this beautiful picture I ascended the
long flight of steps as if approaching an altar. What is it
that suddenly makes the climb so easy for me? What
draws me nearer and nearer to the beloved sight above
me? What is this power that fills me with such awe and
devotion? Is it the sound of the bells that lifts me up? Is it
love for my grandparents that urges me towards them?
What one experiences through movement can never be
expressed in words; in a simple step there may be a
reverence of which we are scarcely aware. Yet through it
something higher than just tenderness and devotion may
flow into us and from us.

Having arrived at the top I stood facing my grandparents.[5] I talked with them about my future for a long
time, until the first stars began to shine. What exactly I
told them has escaped my memory but I can remember
the utter peace and comfort I felt within myself and that
everything was suddenly and completely clear.

My grandfather was delighted with my rather
revolutionary ideas. In the great revolution one of his
forefathers had been a renowned leader of the
bourgeoisie, and because of his political attitude, had
been condemned to death and had had to flee the

[5] They were his mother's parents. His grandfather was a physician and
   surgeon who was in charge of the main Hospital in Budapest. He died in
   1898.

country. This man must have been in my grandfather's mind as he listened to me now, for his face lit up and he said: "I believe this boy has the makings of a politician in him." But my grandmother shook her head sadly and said: "I fear, father, he will become an artist."

My grandparents died soon after. They had departed, according to my great-grandmother to dance on God's meadow, while I was still trying to sort out my doubts and troubles with other experienced people. My mother could not help me either.[6] Unfortunately I saw her very little during my childhood because she was always away with my father in the borderlands and later she had to nurse my sister[7] who was seriously ill for years before she died. My mother was very young when I was born and thus a wonderful relationship developed between us, a comradeship in which I was almost like an older brother. One Christmas long ago when I was staying with my parents I had been able to race her on ice-skates. When I was still quite small her ambition had been to turn me into a competent horseman, swimmer and tennis player, just as she had been encouraged by her father, the physician, to do all sorts of physical exercises.

In later years I spent all my Christmas holidays in the house of my uncle who used to send me to other relatives on Christmas Eve because he liked being alone. With them I was allowed to listen to my host's daughters playing piano duets, I saw an unfamiliar Christmas tree and regularly every year was given a box of writing-paper and a bag of oranges. After this I took my leave as quickly as possible because I felt my presence was rather superfluous. On one of those Christmas Eves I wandered through the streets, saw candle-lit trees everywhere with people happily gathered around them, and I felt that

[6] Laban's mother was a very cultured and progressive society woman. She had great compassion for people less fortunate than herself, sympathised with the socialist outlook and was most generous in giving. So was his father, but his military education and duty made him a severe and conservative man who could not understand Laban's artistic leanings or support him.

[7] Laban was the oldest of four children and the only boy.

there was nobody I could ask for advice. From then on I knew that all my decisions had to be made by myself. "And your father?" asked the Queen of the Night.

My Father taught me the life of a soldier, which fascinated me almost as much as did the arts. He was an officer of high rank, and mostly stationed in distant border garrisons, where there were no suitable schools for my education. I would gladly have done without them. I much preferred taking part in manoeuvres on horseback, and training in fencing, shooting, riding and other forms of sport and combat. Soon I imagined myself a better judge than any staff officer of tactics and strategy, from company and battalion exercises to the manoeuvres of huge corps. It was splendid to see our soldiers spreading out over the hills and fields to bar the enemy's way as they approached out of the distance. Suddenly in a wood to the right of the hill where we were stationed we could see their weapons flashing and then how wonderful it was when my father immediately ordered the artillery into position on the hillside. Horses panted, soldiers surged forward and gun carriages bumped over the field. It was as if everyone was flying and tearing about in wonderful designs and, when the enemy broke out of the woods to storm the hill with bayonets drawn and loud shouts of hurrah, the volley of our gunfire peppered their lines so that as any child could have seen, the cunning attack was beaten off.

Enthusiastically, I told the queen how splendid it was when information came that the enemy had brought up considerable reinforcements behind their left wing and my father gave the command to halt them. Boldly we swooped down on horseback in a broad curve through a covered valley and then made a surprise attack along a wide front. The reinforcements were disarmed and forced to retreat.

I was justifiably proud of my father, who always had to win, of course, and the pleasure I got from my own physical exertions became associated with my admiration for the splendid display of movement. Troop formations on ceremonial occasions, such as parades, march-pasts, musters, and the occasional funeral showed a unity which I assumed could only come about through steady comradeship and loyalty: loyalty of one to another, and of the individual to the whole, to the all-embracing unity, to the fatherland. All this made the civilian look quite pathetically insignificant beside my picture of the professional soldier. Only art matched up to this ideal.

The Queen of the Night listened to me without interrupting.

We then talked of my songs and fairy-tales. She seemed eager to hear and see them and soon after she got a number of people together and invited a woman singer to give a performance of my songs.

To my surprise there was a great deal of applause. The Queen then gave me a room where, with a group of young actors, I was to produce for a charity performance an amusing play which the fashionable poet had written. We were soon at loggerheads during rehearsals, however, because what this man wanted was quite outside my experience. There were scenes from thieves' kitchens, gambling dens and similar places of entertainment which as yet I knew nothing about and the script was laced with mocking allusions to society and the world which were supposed to represent the ideal life of a big city.

Once, when I was sitting in a rather depressed mood, in the ivory-coloured boudoir of my beautiful protectress, she suddenly asked me: "Is your heart really so set on the fairy-tales of your childhood?"

"What do you mean?" I asked, taken aback, "I thought you liked my work!"

She burst out laughing and then looked at me sternly:

"For a beginning it may be quite a good test of talent, but surely, you don't really think that you can build a future on such old-fashioned romanticism!"

The viper-arms played with a shawl and she virtually hissed at me when she spoke again:

"I detest sentimentality, and all your things are frightfully sentimental. Take a thoroughly good look at life! Then you'll soon realise for yourself that something quite different is needed to-day."

With scarcely another word I took my leave. This woman's views had an uncanny influence upon me. My ideas seemed suddenly childish to me, my hopes and aspirations nonsensical. Would I really have to take a different approach to enable me to reach people's hearts? I repeated the conversation to the fashionable poet. "Of course she's right. I wanted to tell you so myself and advise you to have a good look at the world first of all but I didn't feel it my place to do so. Now, since you've broached the subject yourself I'll give you a few tips."

The time which followed was like an awful dream, or, rather, an awful awakening. Together with friends of the goddess, and sometimes with her as well, I crawled around the places of entertainment. I was lent money and people showed great zeal when it came to initiating me into this magnificent kind of life. In one revolting den—in a room next to a gambling club—I met the goddess again. "Well, how's our young friend who makes up fairytales? Here you can really experience them! Ever smoked hashish?" Everybody present rolled their eyes in rapture. Shamefully I had to admit that I had never tasted the stuff, despite my travels to the Orient. The goddess clapped her hands and a negro boy brought the smoking implements. I had to try it, but instead of heavenly visions I experienced such nausea that I had to leave the room. It was just the same with all the pleasures I came across in this company and I considered myself to be terribly boorish.

The queen soon noticed my lack of enthusiasm for her choice of entertainment. She began to tell me of her own dreams and aspirations in the arts, and how at one time she had wanted to become a dancer. Then she suggested showing me some of her dances, so a few days later we met in the same room in which we had rehearsed the play for the charity performance. The pianist sat behind a gold-embroidered silk curtain, and was not allowed to watch. She appeared in very tasteful costumes, and danced exactly like her snake-like arms. I cannot say that I disliked the sinuous movements, which flowed from her finger tips to her toes. On the contrary, there was refinement and meaning in her performance, but her way of moving was so different from what I had considered to be dance until then that I could not restrain myself from making comments. I told her of sword-dances, of dervishes and peasants, of goblins and gods from the mountains, but for an answer she broke into peals of laughter: "That might do for peasants and idiots or for young men, but it doesn't look as though you have ever seen a real woman dance before. There is no need to tell you what my movements express, I couldn't do that anyway, but what you envisage simply isn't art for us."

Again I fell under the spell of this woman and I now tried to look at dance from quite a new angle, namely that of "female feeling." I plunged into the high-life of her court, went to cabarets and similar entertainments though without finding any lasting response within myself. Some things really interested me even though they inwardly repelled me. It was not so much the entertainments themselves but the insights I got into hitherto unknown social strata and conditions which the goddess's hangers-on simply regarded as a form of amusement.

One day, after we had just had a meal with the goddess in a luxurious restaurant, the fashionable uncle asked me to take his latest book to a little shop-girl who lived in a suburb some way out. He added: "You'll get a surprise!" and he was right. I was not only surprised but utterly confused, shocked and horrified. The girl, whom I had seen in his company once before, I now found living in a dilapidated, evil-smelling house in a district blackened by coal-dust. In front of the dark hole which served as an entrance to the house, squatted an older man with an animal expression on his face and a bottle of spirits between his knees. Next to him sat a small, freckled girl, with unpleasantly experienced eyes in her pale little face. They were the father and sister of the shop-girl whom I had come to see. I asked for her and the father called her name in a thick voice. She came to the door chewing a piece of bread and on seeing me at once tried to put on a social manner which reminded me unpleasantly of the movements of my goddess. Into my mind flashed the fashionable uncle and the goddess, the hotel where we had just dined and the waiter, dressed in a coloured tailcoat and knee-breeches who had served delicacies with gloved hands. I was still conscious of the flower-scented air under the palm trees and the bright lights and I felt as if the coal-dust which I was now breathing would suffocate me. Worst of all, however, was the memory of the contemptuous manner of the poet, the malicious smile with which he had accompanied his "You'll get a surprise." In such moments I hated all these people and never wanted to see them again, but the mysterious magic of the Queen of the Night always pulled me back into the vortex. She knew how to fascinate me with her tales of worldly experience—an experience which I had yet to acquire and so my feelings of revulsion continually fluctuated. At the same time, a frightening thought became more and more strongly rooted in my mind: I must create a work which would portray this world at its crudest.

So I began to acquaint myself more closely with other aspects of city life. I went to the stock exchange and watched the excited jobbers pushing and shoving in and out, with fixed stares on their faces, shouting hoarsely and brandishing bits of paper. They would tear these out of each other's hands, career madly about and then collapse in despair in a heap, only to shoot off again hunting for yet another piece of paper. For the first time I also got to know the ugliness of the class struggle. I went eagerly to meetings where platitudes about the differ-ences between the capitalists and the workers were bandied about, where I could see waves of hatred being artificially generated and becoming so real that they were almost physically hanging in the air. Finally, in low-class cabarets I saw poor devils who called themselves artists, and listened to the obscenities with which they fed their audience in order to earn a living. I got to know certain quarters of the city where crime was the order of the day and I caught glimpses of the dark recesses of the souls of many apparently well-bred citizens and saw the inner wretchedness of the wealthy.

It seemed as if from the shadows of large tenement houses, and from the glaring light of streetlamps, new goblins and evil spirits, never seen before, were whirling round me and blotting out all the noble impulses, energy and compassion that man is capable of.

Wasn't the Queen of the Night the ruler of these evil spirits? Wasn't I just bewitched by her glittering green eyes and her viperish arms? Wasn't the perfume of her boudoir like the odour which I had noticed in the mortuary where the bodies of the lost ones were laid out? Didn't this foul atmosphere pollute the whole city and, most of all, every achievement in the arts which the Queen and her followers liked? Wasn't her dancing—that seductive wooing—nothing other than a wish to drag one down into the dark intoxicating nothingness of the night?

Then came the day when in despair I did not know where to turn. My over-excited imagination once again raced ahead of the present. The rottenness and decadence of our so highly-praised culture stared me harshly in the face. A vision took shape within my mind: a dance of the eternally hurrying ones, a dance of the rootless, a dance of the sick cry of longing for lust, a dance of alluring, seductive women, a dance of greed; a chaotic quivering accompanied by crazy laughter. I wanted to drive this vision away but it refused to go. Wasn't it wrong to hold on to this nightmare and wallow in this filth? But the more I tried to free myself the more it worked its way into my imagination. What had the twilight of heart and mind, in which stock jobbers chased one another, waving their papers under their noses in a screaming dance, to do with me? Why should I care for men and women who tried to whip up their wasted senses by all kinds of disgusting means? Why care for the satisfied and the wealthy, who build such a pathetic illusion of happiness with farthings snatched ruthlessly from the poorest, while their own souls wither and perish amid their gilt and opulence? Why should I listen to agitators inciting people to revolt with false blandishments and cunning catch-phrases, perhaps just to make a pile of money for themselves? Has art, so passionately defended as the great provider of happiness and peace, any place amidst this hustle? How can true beauty dwell among the glitter of tattered silk and under the artificial purple lights? How can the soul rejoice amid the rags of the poor and the hollow eyes of hungry children? How utterly remote is the fragrance of the mountains and forests from the air of the slums, so thick with coal-dust and from the deadly smell of the powdered prostitute! Is that the song of man? I wondered in horror.

More than 20 years later, when I returned to these memories, and created my dance-play *The Night*[8] I made the great mistake of expecting too much from my audience. I thought that they, like myself, would have long outgrown the ghastly turmoil of the city's witches-sabbath and would now be able to view a play about such absurd goings on with one eye weeping and the other laughing. But, instead, they appeared to be touched in their secret cravings, and hurt and appalled at the perhaps not too sympathetic way in which I tried to represent with calm detachment the atrocities which had once filled me with so much horror. In any case, I would not class this work as one of my best dance-compositions. In it I showed the violent storms and evil spirits of our time. What the revues and the films of our days made out to be charming and chic, sophisticated and smart, what people took for terribly sweet and amusing, I portrayed here with its true bitter aftertaste, with its obnoxious flavour and its degrading nastiness.

The play opened with a crowd of mechanically grinning society men and women, followed by all I had

[8] *Die Nacht—The Night—*was performaned at the first Dancers' Congress which took place in Magdeburg within the frame of the German Theatre Exhibition, from 21st–24th June 1927. The idea of the Congress was to bring into contact all dancers—*i.e.* dancers of any race and creed—so that, through collaboration, a proper place could be gained for dance amongst the arts. The organising Committee consisted of: Anna Pavlova, Mary Wigman, Rudolf von Laban, Dr. Niedecken-Gebhard (theatre director and manager) and Professor Oskar Schlemmer (from the Bauhaus).

Fig. 3.—The dance of the greedy.

experienced and felt when I first met life in the big city. It was built round a fantasy on work which showed money being earned without work. Greed, covetousness, adoration of three idols: dollars, depravity and deceit. The whole wild orgy found no solution and ended in madness. The music was a caricature of jazz.[9] All this sounds pretty gruesome, and probably it was so. Nevertheless, I must have succeeded in portraying our time, or else the audience would not have reacted with such indignation. It is always tragic when people can no longer laugh at the maze in which they are lost. But also in my play the happy ending was missing. Who could have dared to hope for this in those days?

[9] Erich Ytar Kahn wrote the music for *The Night* following Laban's notation of the rhythms and metres bar by bar. The conductor in Magdeburg was Rudolf Wagner-Regeny.

Chapter 4

THE SORCERER'S APPRENTICE

MEANWHILE, I had become a cadet[1] and had been posted
for a few weeks to the railway workshops, to learn how to
handle machinery and to gain some technical knowledge. At the end of the period a huge farewell celebration was planned for the participants, the officials and the
local dignitaries. My talents had been talked about and I
was asked to arrange the artistic part of the celebration. I
didn't need long to think it over. It seemed a marvellous
opportunity to get my own back on my enemy—the
multi-screwed engine.

At first, I had been thrilled with engines. Visions of the
future—almost entirely realised since then—seemed
utterly out of reach at that time. Aeroplanes, submarines,
radio, television, a proper combustion engine and with it
the automobile, the mastery of electricity, and even the
remote control of ships and instruments were daily
prophesied though most people regarded them as the
wildest fancy.

Strange books came out about Martian man or man of
the future. He was supposed to be nothing but a tangle of
nerves, a kind of brain that sat in a steel capsule and
accomplished the most incredible feats with all sorts of
grabs, feelers and levers.

With strange beams these supermen could saw
through rocks and mountains like butter; they sucked

[1] At the instigation of his father, Laban entered the Officers' Training
Academy in Wiener Neustadt, Austria, where he spent the year 1899–1900.

46

into themselves whatever they liked or could use, and repelled everything that was hostile. Anyone undesirable was grabbed by the leg and hurled into space where he could then compete with the stars in sailing the Heavens and no longer be a burden on earth. The universe as a better Siberia, as the most suitable place for exile, seemed to me an ingenious idea. I don't remember now if I read this somewhere or invented it myself.

In any event, we were still very much at the beginning, and proud of the breech-loading and repeating rifles which could fire several bullets one after another. The construction of machine-guns was just under way but it seemed doubtful whether they could ever be brought into extensive practical use because of overheating and all sorts of other difficulties. In those days the machine-gun was used for honouring royalty. Large targets were set up, and a skilled marksman using the most primitive ammunition would shoot out on to them the name of the person being honoured. It was a harmless practice and one to which even pacifists would not object.

The largest machine-monsters were to be found in the naval arsenals and one of them, which made a very deep impression on me, was a steam-hammer for riveting armour-plates. It was an enormous steel-block that would come crashing down, but it could also be stopped by a hair's breadth so that even a pocket-watch placed underneath could be pinned down but not damaged. However, in this world of steel and in the chemical laboratories where juvenile attempts were made to improve the mediocre effectiveness of explosives, I saw something quite different from what the artillery major expected me to observe.

Machines looked to me like clumsy imitations of animals. The locomotive scrutinised me with bottomless, impersonal eyes. Wasn't its monstrous belly filled with water just as a drunkard's is filled with beer? And didn't the spokes of the wheels propel the monster along just as our legs propel us? The joints are constructed on exactly the same principles as ours. And the fodder that puts fire into the ungainly belly and sets it all into motion! This new animal, born from the brain of man, is a vegetarian which devours carbonised plants, I thought. But doesn't it also devour man? It does not feed on the body, the flesh and the visible form, but on the soul!

I saw with growing clarity how man will come under the domination of the machine. The soul-less steel-ox, the locomotive, is only a beginning. Thrilling as the power of conquest over air and sea may be, man will surely have to pay dearly for it. The whirring and clanking of thousands of wheels and chains is infectious: soon man himself will become a whirring of wheels and chains; soon he will see in life, in the whole of nature, and in himself nothing but the machine, and the soul will be forgotten.

"Cadet, answer me!" shouted the major. But I had not heard his question, I had not been looking at the screws and valves which he was explaining, but at the monster, a new idol, which the sorcerer's apprentice had created. I saw man under the spell of its creature, I saw the fearful, distorted eyes of millions, who could not find the formula for banishing the spirits which they themselves had summoned up.

Wasn't the magic word "Soul"? But hadn't the soul already withered and died in the maze of our spurious culture, in the turmoil of the big city? Wasn't it irreparably and irrevocably lost? Wasn't it the task of the arts to re-awaken it, to keep it alive? And didn't I belong much more to those whose task it was to arouse the soul through their dreams and prayers, than to those who increased the power of the machine by diligently tending its screws and chains?

Of course, both are necessary—skill which fashions tools, and art which builds on dreams; all people who make things are builders and creators of the products of culture. But each of them has his own place. For me it became clear in that machine workshop that my place was not to serve the soul-less steel-ox but rather to become a kind of adversary and antithesis to it, in spite of my admiration for its power.

All this explains why I regarded the steel-ox at the cadet-festival as my enemy, and wanted to make fun of him. A sorcerer's apprentice of a different kind, I wanted to summon up different spirits.

The spirits of heaven and earth, as I saw them in my imagination, are the inexplicable, the unfathomable in nature. The sound of the human voice and the movement of the human body, if rightly used, can alone bring us near to glimpsing these worlds. I have felt the might of the unknown in the mountains, on the sea, and in the land of adventure, and as it has moved me, so it shall move others.

The weakening and languishing of the soul, which I had experienced when I was caught in the net of the Queen of the Night, had to be prevented! But how? And which way to go?

So the festival of the cadets became a welcome occasion to introduce something of this other world into our rattling of wheels.

Happier and easier in my mind than ever, I set to work. At first the hundred comrades from all parts of the Empire[2] who served here with me had no desire to fall in with my plans. But duty was duty and reluctantly they toed the line. I had planned that everyone who came should take part in a dance of joy round a large brand-new locomotive in the engineering workshop, so making real fun of the steel-ox. But it all turned out differently. Apart from the fun, my plan was also to have some typical dances performed in national costume for, without taking any notice of borders, I wanted to show the predominant cultures which we young people represented. I saw it like this. The main element, or at least the language of the army, was German. This naturally called for a waltz. Then there were the Hungarians with their magnificent Czardas and the Slovaks from the south with their national circle dance "the Kolo" which could be very entertaining. The initial reserve gave way to wild enthusiasm, and everybody wanted to bring their national characteristics into the limelight: the Poles their mazurka, the Bohemians their polka, the Styrians their

---

[2] The Austro-Hungarian Empire stretched over the whole of South-East Europe, embracing peoples of a great diversity of races, nationalities, customs and beliefs.

ländler, the Tyrolese their schuhplattler, an Italian a tarantella, a Sevenburger an old nameless peasant dance, the Ruthenians Russian dances and lastly a Herzegovinian a dervish dance.

During the negotiations I began to understand something of the difficulties which must have been encountered by the various privy councillors of conciliation who travelled endlessly from one region to another labouring to maintain an always rather precarious peace and sense of union.

At last we agreed on a dozen basic types of dance and I wanted to pick out the most talented dancers to take part in all the different groups, Slavonic, German, and so on. When I did this it was shattering to see the deeply-rooted differences between individual nationalities coming to light. For each national group I appointed dance-leaders who were well acquainted with the particular type of dance and so everything went fairly smoothly, although there were always some who were unable to adapt themselves to peculiarities of movements that were alien to them.

This difficulty was particularly noticeable with the dervish dances. There was only one man from that region but he was not familiar with the dances, or at least not sufficiently familiar to be a successful leader. Now I have seen dervishes dance more than once during my travels in the land of adventure, but to dance like them is unbelievably difficult.[3]

The dancing dervishes are Moslem lay-brothers who perform their prayers not in words but in body-movements, and especially in endless turnings. Over the years I had become almost indifferent to seeing the Turks attending to their daily prayers, alternately kneeling down and getting to their feet, touching the ground with their foreheads and in this way executing a lengthy prayer exercise. Gaunt old men with long white

---

[3] Laban was fortunate in having been introduced to the ceremonies and exercises of dervishes, which could not be seen publicly, by an Imam under whose protection he travelled as a youth to visit his father. The experience had a lasting influence on his vision of dance.

beards are almost more elastic than the young ones, for their body movements have become completely automatic after decades of practice. The first time I tried to do these prayer exercises, I didn't find them at all easy. Moslems would tell me of their value for the physical health of a person, but the spiritual value supposed to be contained in them was something I could not really appreciate then. As for the dervish-dances they are, at first sight, completely incomprehensible, even almost repulsive in the wild whirling which goes on till the dancers froth at the mouth. It all seems quite mad to us, but it is probably in the madness that the sense lies.

It is impossible, of course, to describe the essence of the movements. But sometimes one can experience the same sort of tremendous impulse to move, for example, in a fight, in danger, in ecstasy and in passion, in short, in times of excessive emotion. The fact that venerable men with long beards can devote themselves to such experiences and even maintain that they do so in honour of God always made me think. But one day on seeing the strange effects of these dances or, rather, how the accompanying state of trance affected the bodily functions of these dervishes, I began to sense their deeper meaning. I saw to my astonishment dervishes, in a state of high ecstasy, driving long needles and nails through their cheeks, and through their chests and their arm muscles, without showing any sign of pain or, even more important, without losing a drop of blood. Afterwards, there was no trace of a wound where the point had penetrated; the muscle-tissues had closed up immediately. When they began to use sharp knives on themselves I was reminded of the assertion of the old mountain peasants that the magic of the dance made the body immune to cuts and thrusts. Indeed some time ago I came upon a mountain village where I saw a very strange dance in progress. Sixteen young men wearing garters with jingling bells round their knees, and carrying swords in their hands were walking round in a circle. The whole thing looked sinister and threatening. They stepped to the beat of drums, which sounded hard and loud in the silence. Otherwise it was deathly quiet, although there were many people standing round. The youths raised their swords with sharp movements and struck them one against the other. Then suddenly every alternate man jumped over the sword of the one in front. They made shapes of stars and crosses with their swords and then struck them again one against the other. Their complete absorption in the dance and the apprehensive way in which the spectators watched every one of their movements was positively uncanny. In a low voice I asked an old man next to me what it all meant. Startled, he motioned me to keep quiet.

The youths then moved away from the dance-square with the same sharp steps. As if relieved and released, the crowd began to chat and laugh.

"There mustn't be any talking during a sword-dance" said the old man at my side. "It brings bad luck."

We soon got into conversation and he seemed very pleased to have found someone to talk to about it. His face lit up as he told me of the time when he himself had taken part in these dances. "But it was quite different in those days—we still believed in it. And women were not allowed to be present. But as it is now," he continued disparagingly, "the magic has no effect."

I asked what kind of magic it was supposed to be.

"Immunity to cuts and thrusts" he whispered. I did not grasp at once what he meant, but then remembered the superstition that there were various ways of making oneself immune to cuts and thrusts and thus of becoming invulnerable. But there was no further information to be got from the old man, not even over a glass of wine which we drank together.

On my way home, I reflected on all this. Belief in a magic that conquers nature was surely just foolishness, a childish superstition—but even so, wasn't there something great, something immense hidden behind it?

Were the dervishes really immune to cuts? Could dancing really have such a power over man?

Many of us may already have experienced how dancing can induce an enhanced, or at least a different kind of consciousness from our normal practical every-day awareness of the world. How far this can go, and whether one can attain extraordinary powers through dance, I could not judge at that time. Here it was simply a miracle that I saw with my own eyes, an unbelievable conquest of nature.

But now what was I to do? I didn't want to abandon the spectacular item of the dervish dances, so I had to rehearse them myself, even if I had no prospect of bringing my flock to a state of invulnerability.

The dagger-dance which the Ruthenians wanted to show also got into difficulties. It was a kind of Cossack-dance, similar to one which I had once seen performed in the south of Russia by a visiting Russian frontier-regiment. Here too, I was able to step in and help to show the steps and draw out of the obstinate performers the character and the necessary temperament for the dance.

I recalled what I had learnt meanwhile about the strange world of sword-dances, youth initiations, and such-like. All dagger- and weapon-dances have their roots in the age-old sword-dances which exist in a similar form among all the peoples and races of the world. They are not just a preparation for fighting: the training of the body in resilience and dexterity, which facilitates the use of weapons, is only of secondary importance in the weapon-dance. It seems that the secret of immunity to cuts and thrusts played a part in all these dances of early times, and in the youth initiation rites of all primitive peoples the magic ceremony, through which the state of invulnerability was reached, played a major part. Youths were also initiated into the magic art of healing. The secret of this is essentially based on the belief that illnesses and wounds cannot only be healed with oint-ments and dressings but also through special methods of controlling the blood circulation. Isn't that also the deeper meaning of the magic dances? North of the Caucasus there are tribes who inflict quite severe injuries upon themselves during the wild dances of their reli-gious ceremonies. Blood flows freely, but afterwards the open wounds close up very quickly. In a normal state the

injuries and loss of blood would have caused deep
fainting fits; but the sword-dancers hardly ever succumb
and dance frenziedly on until they suddenly come to a
halt, wipe off the blood and then go peacefully home.

Sword-dances like all dances of combat, have yet
another meaning and aim. They are the basis for the
rules of fencing, which not only teach the effective use of
weapons, the exploitation and application of all kinds of
feints and ruses but, over and above, lead to good
conduct in battle and to a noble, manly approach to
combat. For, in contrast to bestial outbursts of fury
followed by senseless destruction, there is such a thing as
fair fighting. Bombing houses and burying healthy soldiers, women, children, the old and the crippled beneath
the ruins, is not fair fight. Don't the limits imposed by
nature on human courage and self-control, indicate what
is decent, manly behaviour in battle? Wouldn't it be
helpful to us to clarify these limits through organised
contests and dance-plays as is already done to a certain
extent in sport? Isn't this also the meaning of "sporting
conduct"? When and how may I kill? This is a question
still to be answered. And I thought that dances of combat
could teach us something here.

The dagger-dances of our celebration were only
modest imitations of this splendid art. But all the same,
we strove to bring the spirit of manly conduct, fighting
courage, and daring skill into our performance, and we
succeeded quite well.

Unfortunately, it was out of the question to include
women in our dances so I had the thankless task of
training some of my comrades for the female parts. This
caricature of mixed sex dances was not very satisfactory,
but since nowadays dance and love are more often
associated than dance and combat, the feminine side
could not be left out, even though it had to be done
through more or less successful impersonation.

Finding the music was also not very easy. My dance-
leaders and dancers insisted on their own special national
tunes which I had to guess and arrange sometimes only
from inaccurate whistlings. After a great deal of trouble I

FIG. 4.—Sword-dance.

managed to get the costumes together, over three
hundred of them. But there was no time or money left
for my anti-engine joke. All we did was to cover the
steel-ox with small flags in the colours of the nationalities
involved, and the conquest of mind over matter was
demonstrated only through the human art of movement.

I was thrilled and blissfully happy with my task and
activity. When, after a really handsome performance of
our improvised male ballet, the audience broke into
thunderous applause, and the men from the workshops
who had been allowed into the engine-hall for the
occasion, thanked us with radiant faces, I was simply
carried away. It was very strange that through such a
chance the first fulfilment of a secret wish came true. It
was my first dance production on a larger scale.

Had I not been so young and at the bottom of my heart
so frustrated, I would not have cherished the flattering
compliments for more than they had actually been
intended. The suggestion "you should really have
become a dancing master" I took for praise, when
perhaps it was only said ironically. For the first time in my
life the thought entered my mind that dance was the art
with which I should be involved. Thoughts of immunity
to cuts and thrusts did not come into this, however. On
the contrary, I soon considered these childish ideas as
amusing. Why should one protect oneself against danger
as medieval knights did in their ridiculous suits of
armour? The essence of human magnanimity must lie
somewhere else than in the prevention of injury.

The thought of the magic in dance held fast in my
mind and my decision to give my life to the arts became
irrevocable. The inspiration to compose a play *The
Sorcerer's Apprentice* never took shape, but much later I
introduced fragments of the idea into *The Night*.

Chapter 5

THE TIGER

IN the early days of my career I often had to face hard times. One day in a well-known seaside resort[1] I stood in front of the chief editor of a local German daily newspaper which filled its four pages with the gossip of international idlers.

"The main thing is to give the tiger a taste of blood" said the great man, and with these words he placed a uniform-cap on my head. Then he hung a huge newspaper sack over my shoulder with his own hands and declared that by this simple ceremony I was employed as a newspaper seller in the "X" publishing house and retail business.

I had really come to see this man with quite a different request. I had hoped to find work either as a reporter or designer. However, it turned out that on the "X" paper all the ingenious outpourings, which were signed with all sorts of grandiose names, came purely and simply from the chief editor's pen. The only other person there was an old book-keeper who scrawled away at a stand-up desk and received the rare visitors with a grumpy unwillingness, suspecting every one of them to be a creditor.

[1] This was Nice. Laban had broken away from home and gone to Paris for study and experience. He was without any means but kept himself going by doing a variety of jobs such as drawing caricatures for journals, arranging and performing in small revue-type shows, painting, writing, dancing, and selling newspapers, as here in Nice. He lived in Paris on and off between 1900 and 1907.

They did not need a designer either, and I had no choice but to accept the post of newspaper-seller.

In the evening I met my colleagues, about a dozen of them, when they came to hand in their takings. Some of them I liked at first sight, especially a fat jolly man with a fair moustache, whom I soon came to trust. Others I took to less. A tobacco-chewing loud-mouth who spat all over the place, and a small dark fellow with shifty eyes, who kept transferring things from one pocket to the other, I didn't care for. When it came to paying in my takings it was "Fatty," as everyone called him, who gave me a helping hand, and the grumpy book-keeper seemed to be quite satisfied with my beginner's achievement. Someone pressed my meagre share into my hand and then the stern chief came along and gave out the orders for the next day.

I learnt that a special task had been assigned to me. The first train from Germany arrived daily at three fifty-five in the morning. At four o'clock sharp I was to be in the courtyard of a post-office and scramble up by a drainpipe to a particular window of a raised ground-floor office. There I was to knock on the glass three times softly and significantly. A post office clerk would open it and hand me all the newspapers and magazines that had arrived by the early train. By doing this, the publishing house of "X" was able to flourish all the latest papers as early as seven in the morning when their unsuspecting competitors were still waiting for the post office counters to open. Smiling maliciously, the little dark fellow with the shifty eyes handed me a large leather bag into which I was to stuff the papers as soon as they came and rush them to the editor's office. It was he who had held this honourable post until now.

Next morning, I discovered the meaning of his nasty malicious grin. In other words, the arrangement with the post office was anything but easy. It was simple enough getting into the courtyard and counting up the windows according to instructions: one, two, three, four—and five next to the drainpipe. That was the one. At first sight, even though I was an agile gymnast, it looked quite impossible to climb the flat wall. However, I took a running leap at it and tried to grab hold of the drainpipe and on my third or fourth attempt managed to reach the window. I knocked quickly on the pane. A shadow appeared, nodded to me and withdrew. It felt like an eternity until he came back and I could hardly hang on to the narrow sill a minute longer when at last the window opened and an enormous heap of packages was thrust out at me. Thank God, my leather bag was wide open and most of them fell straight into it. I dropped to the ground and went to the office, quite determined to give up this honourable post for ever. There I was told that fetching the morning mail was always the job of the latest recruit and that refusal to fall in with this custom would be considered most uncomradely. So I complied in the hope that I would soon find a successor. Gradually, I got into the swing of it and managed the morning climb in a few minutes with the confidence of a sportsman. Back at the office I was given my share of newspapers and allowed—with rather aching shoulders at first—to take up my stand in the sunlit sea air.

Not only was it all new to me but it was also amusing to see from quite another side all those elegant people with whom I had previously mixed and experienced such boredom. I saw no-one I knew. Most interesting were the evenings on which "Fatty" took me to the local bar. Sometimes we were just by ourselves, but at others colleagues and even strangers joined us and the air was filled with a kind of raucous gibberish as all the languages mingled together. The conversations were at first quite unintelligible to me, and only now and then could I pick out a few words of languages I knew, spoken mostly by sailors and negroes. For the first time I listened to socialist table-talk and was much surprised at their intricate ways of thinking and extensive knowledge of a literature entirely new to me. I couldn't help thinking that all this twaddle was just as silly and insincere as it had been in the literary drawing-rooms of my earlier social circle. During the course of events through which fate had led me to "X" I had come to know much suffering,

other people's and my own, and I could no longer
imagine that everything was as beautifully and patriarch-
ally arranged as it had seemed at home in my youth. But
here I saw and heard a whole host of new things. Once,
when one of these people recited: "I prefer the dirty
marks on my shirt to the medals on the chest of a
general," I wondered secretly what they would say if they
knew I was the son of a well-known general. However,
they were all remarkably discreet, and observed an
exemplary indifference to the origins and past lives of
those they were with. They hadn't a good word to say
about their bosses, however. "Our old man" they said of
the worthy chief editor of the "X" newspaper "is a dirty
dog. He collects the headings of sold newspapers and
returns them when the accounts are drawn up." For the
purpose of accounts all unsold newspapers had to be
returned to the editor in Germany and in order not to
make the parcels too bulky, only headings were sent. If
headings of already sold papers were included then it
was obviously a fraud. I found this manoeuvre so shock-
ing that they had a job calming me down. They tried to
pass it off as only a rumour, and said that the newspaper
might even fold up if it wasn't done and that we should
after all be thankful for our bread and butter. When I
intimated to "Fatty" that I would ask the book-keeper
outright for an explanation of the business, he answered:
"Leave the old chap alone. He's the best man in the world
and his heart is in the right place."

All the same, one evening I could not resist telling the
book-keeper straight out that I had heard of these
fraudulent practices and that I wanted an explanation.
He looked at me with astonishment and then went on
filling in his books. He seemed to ponder; I waited for an
answer.

"Look here" he said suddenly, "what really made you
come here?" I murmured something about temporary
financial embarrassment.

"You really should learn to make a decent living," he
continued. "Your—forgive my harsh words—very
stupid question shows that you are just a hopeless
idealist, and that never gets anyone on in life."

When I insisted that I was disgusted by such a lack of honesty, he broke in quickly, "All right, calm down. It's all right according to agreements which you know nothing about. But come and see me tonight. I believe there are a few other things we could talk over together." With those words I was dismissed or, at least, he didn't deign to look at me again. I went back to my work feeling rather depressed that perhaps I had done this honest man an injustice.

That evening I turned up punctually at his home. "Come on now, let's hear it. What's on your mind?" It was said in such a kind but firm way that I gave in, and slowly, began to tell him of my doubts about the world in which I tried to make my way as best I could. He was silent for a moment and then looked at me over the rim of his spectacles.

"As you're telling me all this couldn't you also tell me quite frankly what is the matter with you? Did you get yourself into trouble?"

"Yes," I cried, "I lived in such a frightful and dishonest world that I couldn't bear it any longer, and when I ran away, I deceived myself with rubbish about beauty and art until I reached rockbottom. Now I know that there is nothing in all this and—"

"So, you invent new deceptions" he broke in, "you are a dreamer; I could see it straight away in the shape of your head. That's a bad thing. But you still haven't answered my question: what were you doing before now?"

A strange feeling of trust came over me. It was years ago—or even never before—that I had confided my innermost thoughts to anyone. I told him briefly of my youth up to the time of leaving my father's house.

"And you don't want to go back to your parents?"

"No, at least not before I've achieved something."

"I can understand that," he declared and then he was silent for some time. I didn't know whether this signified regret for my stupidity or praise for my endurance. When he noticed my own silence he muttered quickly: "Go on, tell me some more."

Haltingly, I came to the hard times which had led me in the end to "X."

"Things went quite well at first. Sometimes I was invited to show my talents. But I hadn't learnt how to earn money. I was even ashamed to accept money for my work. Whereas previously I had been too proud to give up a horse of my own and a servant for the sake of art, now I suddenly had to learn that it was even more difficult to miss several meals in a row. I never have learnt how to handle money!"

"I should think that's the worst thing of all you've told me," he remarked.

"In spite of some lucky chances which always brought me work and success, I got more and more miserable. But the real trouble was the tremendous inner disillusion which came upon me when I became aware of the artificial culture in which we live."

"Heavens, what crazy demands you make on people! They are not angels and never will be!"

I disagreed: "An artist who has noble feelings should not go along with the falsehoods and deceptions of his time. It is essential for men to aspire to be angels, even if they can never reach those heights."

"I think you will eventually see that your sentimental notions are based on false assumptions."

"I already have seen that, but then I fell into the opposite trap and began to detest society as a whole."

"All this to-ing and fro-ing will come to a sticky end," he growled.

"If only I had not gone through these frightful experiences which influenced me so much and completely cut me off from the arts although inwardly I am still bound to them."

"Life certainly is a battle. You simply have to fight—and I mean fight."

"Oh, you've no idea how hard I've fought. I've defended artists with my fists when they were insulted because, in spite of everything, I rated them more highly than the rest of the rabble. Once, when I mentioned that I wanted to become a dancer someone made derisive remarks. I challenged him and he then told me to my face in a most abusive manner what he thought of dancers of both sexes. Up till then my behaviour and strong appearance had saved me from being told such things. But this fellow wouldn't stop and his insults got more and more offensive. Unfortunately, I've always been hot-tempered and we were soon on the floor and rolling about in a disorganised scuffle. He was big, strong and agile so I had to put everything I'd got into it. But suddenly he fell back unconscious under the table. My colleagues pulled me away. I was badly battered myself. My clothes were in shreds, and my face and hands were deeply cut from bits of broken glass that were scattered all over the place. To this day I don't know if I was more inwardly tormented at the thought of being arrested for murder, and thus disgracing my father's name, or at the bitter realisation that I'd set my heart on the most despised profession in the world. For almost a week I walked about in a daze. Every policeman looked suspiciously at me, which was no wonder considering my scratched face. I didn't dare ask if the man was really dead and then one day I saw him sitting in a coffee-house, with his arm in a sling. I'm ashamed to admit that I felt heartily sorry not to have done a better job. Such vermin should be crushed underfoot. However, he lived and I fear that his kind will live for ever."

"And so you call a rough house like that a fight? But carry on with your story."

"Dancing was finished for me, anyway. I couldn't be part of it any more. What follows is the unhappiest chapter of my life. It wasn't just because I was often in desperate need of basic essentials and simply had to keep my head above water, but because of a tremendous longing for my dreams to come true although I could no longer see a way. I had nothing to hope from the theatre. I knew that from my earliest youth. Unconventional ideas and opinions are rejected from the outset. Morally the theatre is certainly on a rather higher plane than the little places where dancers mostly earn their living. But at least in these places they appreciate original ideas."

"But now do tell me what your future plans are. You really can't go on living in this disorganised way!"

"I'm determined to give up every artistic activity until I'm in a position—if ever—to set up my own establishment where my ideas can materialise as I want them to. The problem is how to get there without funds, experience, or any one to advise me? People from whom I'd hoped to receive advice and help can't even understand my ideas and at best just turn away with a shrug of their shoulders, if they don't actually laugh at me. The only good thing is that I learnt enough from my old friend, the painter, to be able to do a bit of painting."

"Wouldn't it be worthwhile trying to make a go of that?"

"I haven't any talent for it. The only things I can do are caricatures. Caricature suits my present mood too. The world is a madhouse, anyway, and the only sensible thing is to poke fun at it."

"There you are—lying again. Secretly your mind is still set on dance." Crestfallen I had to admit that he was right.

"But I still want to know how you came to us here."

"I used to get recommended from one place to another as a designer. Eventually I turned up here, completely broke, and hoped to get a job as a designer or reporter on your paper. The old man—I beg your pardon—the chief, talked me into selling newspapers. He mentioned something about a tiger who had to get a taste of blood—or what have you—and now I am tasting blood."

The book-keeper paced up and down the room. Then at last he stood still in front of me.

"Quite clearly, the first thing for you to do is to learn book-keeping to get some order into your head. Listen," he continued, raising his voice, "I have an old friend, also German, who I'll have a word with and she will teach you for very little money. I know nothing about your dancing, and I haven't even seen it, of course. But one thing I do know: without book-keeping you won't get any order into dancing either."

So I learnt book-keeping. A kindly, white-haired old lady took great trouble to teach me both accountancy and calligraphy. I had to calculate in Dutch guilders imaginary sales of countless sacks of coffee and convert the totals into other currencies. It was agonisingly difficult and all my wages went on replacing messed-up paper. My nights were no longer spent brooding over the horrible darkness of the big city; instead, I filled imaginary cheques with enormous figures, and debited accounts of legendary Smiths and Joneses. In the day-time I carried round the tiger's belly-bag, full of the most glamorous fashion magazines and brain-products from Germany and sold them along the sea-front. The great snake was dotted with gleaming yachts.

Meeting "Fatty" at the local bar one night I said to him: "You're quite right, the old book-keeper has his heart in the right place." I wondered how I could show my gratitude to this man and give him pleasure. The idea came into my mind of arranging an unusual kind of celebration for him and my white-haired teacher. I got some of my younger colleagues together and concocted a light-hearted play from my joys and misfortunes at the "X" publishing company. They brought a few young working girls along in the evenings. I put my whole heart into giving them lessons in movement on the flat roof of our office-building. The news spread about and soon a crowd of enthusiasts came and joined in. For the first time I began to have ideas, though still rather hazy ones, of something that was much later recalled in my choirs.

The celebration which I called *The Festival of the Tiger* was a great success, for both my two dear old guests of honour never stopped laughing and marvelling at it. I carried on with my movement classes until the course in book-keeping was finished and the holiday season over. My most wonderful reward was to see the young people blossom out; their eyes brightened and new interests were awakened. They, and I with them, forgot petty troubles and we all took great delight in our practices together. Most of them left at the end of the season but several kept in touch with me over the years and told me how they went on practising the exercises regularly and how they enjoyed them.

FIG. 5.—Stargazer and the moon.

Already at that time, my mind was occupied with the idea of composing works in praise of the community and of dancing together. But much time had to pass before this branch of my chosen activity could bear fruit.

Chapter 6

THE FIDDLER

MY first work composed simply and solely for dance was *The Fiddler*. Soon after the book-keeping course was finished and I had said good-bye to my first movement group I set out on my travels again.

After those hard years of struggle I experienced an improvement both within myself and in my circumstances, which enabled me once again to spend a few happy months in the open country.

I went away into the heathlands[1] and there met with people and scenery of rare peacefulness and amazing gentleness, two qualities which have always attracted me strongly. More than once life among peasants had given me not only refreshment but also opportunity for reflection on my own thoughts and feelings. Never before had I been to a countryside to which I responded as deeply as to this heath with its quiet, almost deserted villages, and its bright, sandy paths leading across the waving blooms to far-away blue hills. These serene people who moved firmly but simply through days of work and days of rest lived in proud and happy seclusion, comparable only to the dreamy atmosphere of a fairy-tale. The peasant was a kingly figure who, without an inn sign or a licence, took

[1] Laban went to the heaths of the Weserland in Germany, North of Hanover, the homeland of his first wife, Martha. She was also a painter and went back with him to Paris and Nice. They had two children. In this chapter Laban reminisces about his romantic feelings and the sadness on her early death in 1907.

people in from time to time. When I walked into his
room, he nodded silently and went on sitting near the big
tiled stove smoking his pipe. It did not occur to him to ask
what I wanted or to offer me anything. I just walked in
and was at home. The peasant's wife, who appeared
later, also said nothing. After some time when I
announced that I was hungry, she said in low German
which I cannot exactly recall "Well, well, he wants a bite
to eat." It was just the same when I wanted to go to bed.
The way in which everything was offered—with
such spontaneity and generosity—cannot be put into
words. It was like the quiet walks in my grandparents' vineyards, like the circling of eagles in a land of
silence.

Under its white sunbonnet the most lovely face of a
young woman, from whom I was asked to collect two
baskets of apples, was the face of a princess out of the
sagas of old. Her blue eyes spoke gentleness and open-
ness, qualities which had blossomed and ripened on the
lonely heather-farm and were to be found nowhere else.
Nearby was a great island of beech trees, many hundreds
of years old, surrounded by a brown sea of heather not
yet in flower. Large leaves, green weed on the pond over
which echoed the voice of Unkebrunk, king of the toads,
silvery mass of fir-tree thickets, where fairy-tale birds and
sunspots darted about, endlessly racing each other.

And then there was the fair: between wooden stalls
red, green and black dresses, the colours of the bells and
tufts of heather; people engrossed in viewing and
buying; the great empty hall, and right at the back, a few
boards laid across barrels. On them a double-bass, a
fiddle and a clarinet. In the centre of the hall, looking
small and lost, a few couples turning in a simple dance.
My princess from the heather-farm was also among
them. She did not usually mix with people but I had
begged her to come so that we could dance together, and
in her festive dress she moved as freely and unconcer-
nedly as when she was picking apples. She was filled with
the mild sun of the north, and a soft, cool remoteness
floated over her natural gaiety like the mist which

sometimes shrouds the glistening sandpaths of the heather-land in the mornings.

It seemed almost blasphemous to dream of fairy-tale plays here but I could not help it. I told my princess of my experiences in the forest.

In the forest I met two old acquaintances, two mandrakes. Mandrakes are usually very tiny, but these stood big and broad in the undergrowth, their hair shaggy, their faces grinning. Indulgently they let the sunlight dapple their grey-green bodies. You can't talk to mandrakes and their kind as to ordinary people; you have to sing and whistle to be understood. I did this as hard as I could which made them grin even more, and one even shook with laughter.

Suddenly, as from nowhere, a girl leapt out from behind a bush. I had known her for a long time, for she had often come to me in my dreams. Her hair and dress were covered with long, silvery threads, enveloping her like a cloud. They stood out all round her like the fluff of a ripe dandelion. Inside this fine-spun ball one could see the form of a delicately built little body. Every movement was accompanied by a tinkling sound. The many silver threads of her garment rang out like silver bells and I played a few notes on my fiddle in answer to them. From the deep tones of the violin rose a song of great yearning with which the delicate tinkling of the flower-princess intermingled. A large bumble bee kept buzzing angrily between us, obviously annoyed that a human being had dared to invade the land of wood-sprites. Animals peered wonderingly from behind bushes, and the mandrakes had suddenly vanished. From far away came the sound of humming and calling and as it drew nearer I could hear distinctly the repeated call: "Unkebrunk, Unkebrunk." There were sounds of shuffling and sauntering behind the trees. "Save yourself" chimed the bobbing threads on the dress of my princess, "Save yourself. The mandrakes, those treacherous creatures, have betrayed us; my father King Unkebrunk is coming with all his followers." I took up my fiddle again and my happy song drowned the humming and rumbling of Unkebrunk's Court. Suddenly the flower-fairy near me

vanished, and only a shimmering cobweb glistened in the
trembling leaves of the bushes. As if from far away I
heard a faint sound. Wasn't it saying, "Save yourself, for
me"?

At that moment a wind blew up. The massive high
tree-wall all around the glade bent down with curiosity.
"He'll soon get him," whispered the tree-giants, swaying.
"Unkebrunk has never let anyone who trespassed into
his realm escape." I fled through the clearing with frantic
leaps, closing my eyes, shutting my ears with my hands. I
neither could nor would see or hear any more. I wanted
to get away, to people, to people like myself. I didn't want
to fiddle or whistle any longer, but shout, cry, if only to
hear a human voice. At the edge of the clearing I
plunged into the thicket. But what has happened to me? I
can't move, my arms are pinned to my body, my legs are
trapped. Am I caught in this devilish undergrowth?
Suddenly, I see, on my right and my left, half hidden in
the bushes, the two grinning mandrakes. Again, one of
them begins to shake with laughter, holding his dirty-
grey belly with his two wretched root-hands. I can't stop
to quarrel with them because from all sides and from
below I am being grabbed and pulled deeper into the
woods.

In a dark, dank place stands a circle of gloomy fir-trees,
and, on one side, a lone huge beech-tree towers over
them. Again I hear murmuring "Unkebrunk, Unkebrunk." It comes nearer and nearer. Suddenly the fir-
branches part and a few red and blue sprites come
tumbling out. They surround me inquisitively, gleefully.
But I have no time at all to deal with them, because the
fir-trees part again and a whole column of mandrakes
stumps out. Two of them carry a broad golden throne.
All bow deeply, for now King Unkebrunk appears. A
huge toad's head sits on his thick-set body and on it he
wears a delicate crown of forget-me-nots. He seats himself with dignity on the golden throne which the mandrakes have put near the beech-tree trunk.

The two creatures who had so cunningly captured me
were now telling the king with comic bows of all my
misdeeds. They told him how I had trespassed into the

realm of the forest spirits, and how I had bewitched his daughter with my songs of yearning until she responded with a dance of her bells. Unkebrunk jumped to his feet in a rage and sent several sprites off to fetch his daughter. She was obviously going to be forced to watch my doom because two of the dark mandrakes emerged from the background carrying long raspberry creepers and busied themselves putting them around my neck. At the same time they looked up forebodingly at a thick beech branch which jutted out into the dark circle of firs. By now all kinds of woodland creatures had gathered round; they were jumping and fluttering everywhere, under and between the boughs, and creeping on to the branches, so that the firs soon looked like big, richly decorated Christmas trees. A cheeky coloured bird perched on my shoulder and chirped into my ear: "Play them a tune, play them a tune!" Then he flew twittering on to the high beech branch, which was apparently going to be my gallows.

Suddenly an idea came to my rescue. While Unkebrunk was considering me closely from all angles with his glassy, protruding eyes, I started to whistle my tune, trying to imply that I wanted to play just once more on my fiddle. The king understood the message. My last wish was to be fulfilled. Perhaps he was also curious to hear these strange sounds and evidently it never crossed his mind that I might escape between the fir trees, which were crowded with his people. So he ordered me to be released from my fetters and then sat back comfortably in his chair. A mandrake walked solemnly towards me, bowed deeply and handed me my fiddle. My first tune was a merry dance to which the onlookers in the trees began to hop about in delight. Then, slowly and firmly, I began to play my song of yearning, which in the darkness of the forest sounded almost as deep and solemn as an organ. My playing became more and more bewitching, the organ-like sound more intoxicating, Unkebrunk and his people began to blink with tiredness and one after another their heads nodded until in the end the whole forest was snoring like a saw-mill.

Intent only on escaping, I did not notice a delicate white ball appearing high above me, between the trees, and floating down to the ground in front of me like a loose spider's web. It was my flower princess who, attracted by the sound of my violin, had come down into the darkness of the firs. At first she did not see the dangerous company we were in because she was still blinded by the light of the sky. But when she saw her snoring father and all the forest creatures round about me, she was terrified. Timidly she sought refuge with me, then raised herself quickly into the air a little and tried to pull me up with her. But my earthly weight was too much for her delicate substance. I wanted her to fly upwards without me, so that at least she would be saved from the wrath of her kingly father, for Unkebrunk seemed to be coming to life again. He was already stretching suspiciously. The princess clung even more closely to me. We looked around, but there was no chance of escaping with all those creatures massed about us. Not even a sparrow could have slipped through, let alone a human being. Our unselfish struggle in which I wanted to save her, and she was determined not to leave me, was like a dance. When I saw my flower princess floating round me, I felt I must play a really merry song to accompany her and I forgot everything that was going on around me. All of a sudden I noticed how Unkebrunk, rocking to and fro in his half-sleep, was beginning to smile. His whole court were doing the same. When I realised the effect of my tune I played faster and faster and more wildly than ever. The tinkling of the silver threads on my princess's dress mingled with the frenzied music. The creatures and the mandrakes began to lift their stiff limbs and they all started to stretch and shake themselves. The coloured bird hopped hither and thither on one leg on my gallows-branch. Unkebrunk got up from his throne and, slowly turning his clumsy body, he filled the whole place of judgment with his movements. But then he was exhausted and began to puff and pant which made the birds and the other creatures come tumbling down head over heels from the branches of the black fir trees. Now we could escape, the princess and I, from the gloomy circle. We danced out into the clearing. At first we feared that all the forest scoundrels would rush angrily after us, but they stayed behind merry and contented. Unkebrunk, supported by the mandrakes, came tottering and grinning after us, and then, spellbound by my music, the whole train of woodland creatures followed romping through the astonished forest in a long snake. "Now, who would have thought" waved the tree-giants of the glade to one another, "that the fiddler would one day become the son-in-law of Unkebrunk."

This was the play with which I entertained the guests at a wedding in the heath-lands. Peasant boys and girls danced the woodland creatures. The old musician from the tavern lent me his violin. I danced the fiddler.

Many years later this dance became a stage-play and I wrote the music for it myself. Many things had changed—in the play as well as in life. The greatest of our dancers, who came from the heath-lands,—danced in it.[2]

The fairy-tale of Unkebrunk's little daughter is for me not only the symbol of a reaction which brought me to the hilly heaths and forests of the north. It is also a memory of the happiest time of my life and a memory of the sad fading and dying of a being who should never have gone out into the wide world of the restless.

[2] *Der Spielmann—The Fiddler—* was performed in Zürich in 1916. Mary Wigman, still at the beginning of her career, was one of the dancers. She was born in Hanover.

PART TWO

PART TWO

Chapter 1

THE SWINGING TEMPLE

SHROVE-TUESDAY marked the end of the artists' festivals, thank heaven. Working for Carnivals had exhausted me so much that I felt I had to have a break before starting work again. To get away, out of town, was my only wish. The last festivity had been on Shrovetide-Monday and had lasted until the small hours of the morning, for people kept on coming up to talk to me and every time I tried to leave I was delayed by acquaintances or colleagues. At last I managed to escape out into the grey morning. In spite of my patent-leather shoes and silk socks I decided to go straight to the station and catch the next train to anywhere. In the booking hall I could see that the first one was heading for the mountains. I was just in time to jump in, and after a short journey I was in the open air, in the sun and the snow and there were no people. I breathed a wonderful sigh of relief.[1]

Soon the main road grew too monotonous for my liking, so I cut through fields and up a steep hill, often wading above my knees in snow. The exertion made me

[1] Munich, before World War I, was the scene not only of the most lively controversies and progressive thought in the arts in Europe but also a city which pursued its festivals with exuberant mirth. During Shrove-tide one great festivity would follow hot on the heels of the other and artists and laymen took pride in preparing original decorations and spectacular performances. Laban lived and worked in Munich from approximately 1908, painting and experimenting with movement in *Tanz—Ton— Wort* (dance—sound—word) and getting up many of these festivals, particularly in the winter seasons 1911–1914.

feel happy. After all the smooth parquet floors, the dust and the clamour, once again there were trees and earth, rocks and silence, and a clear sky above me. In the late afternoon I came to an inn where I was able to dry my things. Then some peasants arrived for a dance. I sat down with my mug of beer opposite an old forester. Out of a wild beard a nose projected boldly in the middle of a sinewy face which seemed to be carved out of wood. But most striking were the two steel-hard, gleaming blue eyes. They scrutinised me with such detached shrewdness and amusement that I could hardly return their stare. How many thousands of eyes I had had to look into these last days when I called out instructions to crowds of people and had to come to an understanding with them. How many merry, drunken, melancholy and amazed eyes I had seen! And how dull and restless they all seemed now in contrast to the clear, strong gaze of the forester. The innkeeper's wife too and the young couple who sat hand in hand on a bench, the trumpeter who was just shaking the spittle from his instrument, all had this same clear radiance in their faces. What gentle joy and kindness they expressed and how composed they were as they awaited the evening's festivities. Then a schuhplattler dance started up. For me it was just as if I had never seen either schuhplattler or indeed any other dance before. Each movement was filled through and through with lively enjoyment.

With every lift of the knee one could see the delight felt first with the lifting movement and then with the stamping on the floor. Like someone tackling a job with eagerness, here they eagerly got down to the job of dancing. There was no trace of flirtatious affection, only enjoyment of what they were doing. The women whirled round almost like marionettes, their solid ankles seeming to turn the dance-floor, and yet they danced with ease. In the centre the dance-leader, who wore a hat with a yard-long pheasant feather flapping from it, was a virtuoso in sharply articulated jumping and clapping. His movements really sparkled with tremendous speed and variety and rang out like gun-fire, while his expression

showed at once childlike delight and knife-sharp penetration. It was as if they took their dancing as solemnly
and seriously as their prayers, a clear-cut piece of work to
be done with complete absorption. No trace of uncertainty or wantonness, no letting go, no exaggeration,
aggression, or confusion. A wonderful manifestation of
vitality; at the same time there was the great calmness of
the spectators, who stood like rocks, or trees with snow-
laden branches. Stronger than an animal it was, for in
this sense animals do not dance.

The music broke off as if everyone had suddenly got
tired of the whole thing. Back to the benches, to the beer
mugs and long draughts of beer while some of them eye
me suspiciously. What does the pale-face, the city-
dweller, the unbeliever, the bleary-eyed want with nature, with the earth and with this shining life? He belongs
to the pallid, emaciated town. But let him sit and smoke
his miserable cigarettes. I certainly could not compete
with their pipes. Massive clouds of smoke poured from
them as from lots of noisy little locomotives. A large gulp,
a flick of the throat and half the tankard was empty. The
barmaid seizes my tankard from which I have only
sipped—good luck! and the rest has gone. Good luck!

Swiftly, but with restraint the dance begins again. In
their group the dancers look like a machine which works
methodically, and vigorously at this rousing prayer.
Despite their piercing cries they remain faultlessly exact
and apparently detached. Yet, individual characteristics
become even more sharply defined, and in spite of this,
the common ones grow stronger. It is something quite
different from abandonment or ecstasy, a far more
profound experience, something larger than life which
slowly becomes threatening. And over everything, like a
huge demon, hangs a cloud of intoxicating smoke. The
men whip up the women's skirts with light movements of
the arms, like children spinning tops. No surreptitious
glances search for hidden attractions. Everything is
natural and open. Then the music sounds shrill, muffled,
and sharp. A few times more the dance stops and starts
and then it is impossible to see anything. The air is thick

with tobacco-smoke. At first it was only drifting clouds but now it has turned into a solid wall through which figures appear and disappear as if by magic. Two lads jostle each other. The landlord rolls up his sleeves. Most of the men get up and tighten their belts. The women climb on to the benches along the walls and then a fat, red paw grabs my comparatively slender wrist: "Come along, little one, there's going to be a fight!" says the landlady gently, and she pulls me towards a heavy oak-door and from there across a passage to the staircase. Behind me I can still hear a sympathetic "It's nought for townsfolk." Dejected I want to contradict. Why am I not worthy of taking part in this festivity? At the same time I feel too dazed and tired from the exertions of the last few days, from the change of air, the beer, the smoke and the bewildering display of such amazing strength and exuberance. The landlady lights the way up to my room. I follow without a will of my own and soon sink into a deep sleep.

Ash Wednesday was a fine day. Everywhere one could sense that nature was stirring and spring was coming. The confused dreams of the past weeks, from which I had only just awakened, seemed to belong to years gone by. Thank goodness, carnival was over and another immersion into such wild frenzies was out of the question. But I had now to think of leading my helpers and pupils towards some new activities if we intended staying together at all.

I reflected: What had we achieved so far? The memorable carnival festivals, which were later said to have shown the way to a new German stage-art,[2] had culminated in a confrontation between the witches-sabbath of a metropolis and the witches-sabbath of unspoilt nature. The eight hundred performers, who obediently waited on the cold staircase behind the stage until all the spectators and finally members of the court had arrived,

[2] Hans Brandenburg, who in those days was the foremost writer on dance in Germany, wrote in the papers of distant industrial regions about these festivals: "From pure and unassuming indications one can see to-day the beginning of a new birth of the theatre."

filled a huge contraption—the jaws of hell—with a fantastic swarm of giants, demons, witches, dwarfs and every
conceivable fairy-tale creature. The tongue in the hell-
jaws was a chute which passed between sharp teeth
jutting out into the hall like stalagmites. All the eerie
creatures came shooting down this tongue and with them
some characters from the big city, led by the devil, of
course. Around them on the fringe played the harmless
creatures of nature and the clash between these two
worlds ended in the taming of the evil spirits. Even the
devil's grandmother had to turn into a beautiful maiden
and it was she who began a dance in which everyone
joined, spectators as well as the company. The variety of
our dance inventions and the peculiarities of our music
which foreshadowed future artistic developments were
hailed by our contemporaries with storms of enthusiasm.
As a result, no festivals took place at which we were not
present with our dances and other artistic contributions.
As I was in charge of all the stage directions and
constantly had to think up new ideas, I had literally not a
moment's peace for weeks on end.

Another play:

I was also invited by the physicians to direct their
festival[3] and I devised a play from which the whole of the
doctors' entertainment took its name. It was called *In the
Grove of the Aesculapins* and it took place in the shade of
trees before the altar of the god of the physicians. The
doctors appeared as priests and tried to comfort a crowd
of sick and suffering people who were lying about on the
ground in a huge half-circle. They went through marvellous ceremonies and prayer exercises, but these
brought no relief to the afflicted. Accompanying the
doctor-gods were Greek goddesses who threw huge dice
to try to diagnose what was really wrong with the
patients. Then assistants of the healing-priests arrived,
with giant pill-boxes and medicine bottles, but still the
invalids only grew weaker and weaker. At last there
entered a bar-maid bearing as many tankards of beer as

[3] The *Ballo Medico*.

she could carry, and a women with giant radishes and another with Pretzels. They distributed their gifts among the sick and, lo and behold, the lame threw away their crutches, the blind regained their sight and everyone joined in a dance of joy in which the physician-priests fared rather badly. Described in words this must sound like a rather crude leg-pull about a very dignified and worthy profession. But it was well structured as a dance-play and earned a great deal of applause.

The dance compositions had mostly to be worked out at night, and then there were the stage directions, the costumes and everything else connected with them. It was a colossal task. Usually I gathered hundreds of people together and organised them into groups with the help of assistants. Some of these afterwards became well-known dancers. The participants were very con-scientiously trained, but for particularly demanding dancing parts, professionals were called in. Our large halls were not big enough for so many performers so we could only work in groups. It was bitterly cold, with snow falling on the first day of Shrove-tide as if it was the middle of the severest winter, but our performers would stand in touching readiness sometimes through half the night in the snow, forming queues outside our gates, according to police-instructions. When at last their turn came we could not stand on ceremony very much but simply call out: "Shoes off!" "Ladies, corsets off!" "Bend your knees!" "Walk!" "Run!" and then have the neces-sary rehearsal of the steps and gestures, until it was time for the next group of a hundred to come on. And so it continued for weeks, all through the nights, interrupted only by the festival itself and repeat performances. For every festival was put on at least twice. The days were filled with the enormous tasks of making and fitting costumes, and with music rehearsals in which the orchestra had to be inspired and induced into producing musical extravaganzas.

Then the next festival was upon us with fresh perfor-mers. Old ones, ugly ones, crooked ones, awkward ones and unmusical ones, all had to be coaxed into the background with humour, tricks and cunning. The ambitious burst into tears and had to be consoled, and the indignant had to be brought to their senses with humour. Small accidents called for care and help, and in short, not only the first but every festival was a witches-sabbath. Sleep was almost out of the question and eating and drinking were only possible after a performance if we could manage it at all between the congratulations and tributes paid by committees, royalty, public authorities, the press and other interested people. When this was over we, the performers, had to dance with innumerable admirers but we could not really enjoy it after all our exertions. Sometimes we would pack tightly into horse-drawn cabs to attend small private parties and celebrations where yet again all sorts of dances were improvised. Our present greatest and most celebrated female dancers,[4] who had by then already joined my circle, often performed extraordinary and unusual feats. Once, during a wild night in a doctor's house, one of the women artists found a skeleton and improvised a weird duet with its skull. Everyone was deeply moved. The gaiety died down and we all experienced the sense that dance can have another side. In all this there were only indications of hidden visions—no more. It was good to see dance capturing the general public in this way, but I wondered about the young artists. Would they be able to find in this turmoil the love of work, and loyalty to it on which alone they could build their creative work?

For the first time I became aware of my responsibility for this group of people who had put their trust in me. Until then my thoughts had been almost exclusively concerned with my own compositions which grew out of my experiences, sometimes like weeds and at others like slowly blossoming flowers, More often than not I could produce only fragments of my ideas, and even then their

[4] Mary Wigman and Suzanne Perrottet, both originally pupils of Jacques-Dalcroze, had joined Laban in 1913. There were also Gertrud Leistikow, Clothilde von Derp, Alexander Sacharoff and many other young dancers searching for new ways who made their first public appearance in Munich at this time.

faithful reproduction foundered because I had to draw
in people fairly indiscriminately as performers. Also the
environment in which these people lived and worked
made it difficult for them to do justice to the tasks I set
them. I remembered my own development and the
confusion which city-life and the struggle for existence
had brought into my feeling and thinking and I resolved
to do all I could to smooth the way for my young
colleagues by procuring better conditions for the
development of their artistic abilities. During the past
winter I had earned quite a large sum of money, at least
enough for the new task I had set myself if it could be
done on modest lines. Above all else, I said to myself, they
must get out of town and live a totally different life.
Alongside the arts they must do a healthy job, preferably
farming, gardening or something of that kind, for in
both form and content the artistic work must grow out of
the community in which I should like to bring them
together.

I returned to the city and told them my new plans.
What I said was roughly this: that in my opinion man's
real purpose was to create a life with festive occasions;
not festive in the sense of luxurious or idle but as a way of
building up a strong personality and of rising into those
spheres which distinguish man from animal. The great
festivals in life as well as the daily festive moments should
be filled with a spiritual attitude which should concentrate on deepening the sense of mutuality and the
appreciation of the personal identity of each individual.
For this reason, and not out of any contempt for worldly
goods and pleasures, I considered a simple style of living
one of the most important sources of human happiness.
A person who spends too much time and energy on
arranging the details of the material things of life, of his
house, clothes, food and other needs, has neither time
nor energy to participate creatively in this great community idea and in the festive spirit which should be the
goal and supreme aspiration of every culture. Although I
had not previously considered that these ideas had any
general validity, they had nevertheless always been my

own guideline: as little as possible for personal everyday
living which should, however, be organised in a completely modern way, and as much as possible for the daily
building up of the communal culture which should
culminate in festivities and celebrations and be intimately
bound up with the development of the self. I had no
doubt that the performing artist in particular, and even
more so the dancer, could only fulfil his task in a deeper
sense if he considered all his ways and actions to be
preparation and part of festive culture. Although these
ideas were essential to our art, we were certainly not
strong enough to put them into practice as individuals,
and for this reason we had to work together. Therefore, I
asked all those who were in sympathy with my views to
come and help to realise this dreamed-of way of life
somewhere in the open country. The idea met with an
enthusiastic welcome from some of them—it was only
natural that the wheat would be sifted from the
chaff—and so we set out to found our dance-farm.

Summer-festivals were to be our financial backbone
and I made all the necessary preparations for them. A
former vegetarian colony[5] with its small wooden huts
gave us suitable, cheap accommodation, sunbathing
places, meadows, indeed a little kingdom, to which we
added buildings which we ourselves constructed, completed and embellished. Each morning from the veranda
of my small house with its overhanging creepers I
sounded a gong and everyone turned up for work. Tools

[5] This was the well-known colony on the Monte Verità in Ascona, Ticino,
Switzerland, where prominent people of the European intelligentsia,
artists, writers, philosophers, etc. used to go. From 1912 onwards Laban
went there for the summer months with his pupils. From the very beginning
he endeavoured to bring his dancers out into the open air for training so
that their movements would become freer, bigger and more beautiful. His
dream was to set up a dance-farm and, although he did not succeed in
establishing one permanently, there were several periods during which he
came near his goal. For instance, these summers in Ascona up to World War
I, then in 1915–16 at Hombrechtikon near Zürich, in 1920–21 at Cannstadt
near Stuttgart, in 1922–23 at Gleschendorf near Lübeck. The rehearsals for
his stage performances Laban, of course, always conducted in a studio.
Therefore, for the summer months he tried to find places which offered
both suitable indoor and outdoor facilities.

were distributed and before breakfast groups went to the various gardens to weed, dig, plant and do other necessary jobs. Groups of women went into the sewing rooms, where they made dance-costumes and sandals. We had a bakery and later even two weaver's looms which produced the fabrics we needed. Fruit was preserved and meals prepared and cooked in various shifts. However, our main concern was with the places for dancing. In the beginning, we used the existing lawns and later these were fenced in and surrounded by seats. We also planned a beautiful building which would serve a dual purpose by having one half covered for use in bad weather and the other half open to the sky for fine days.

There we planned and performed a dance version of the age-old tale of Ishtar's journey to Hades. Ishtar's journey to the underworld is really a sunset myth but it has a distinctive spiritual content. At each of the seven gates of Hades, Ishtar, the queen, removes an ornament or garment until she stands a simple human being, naked and unadorned, before the last gate. In my dance interpretation the wordly cast-off possessions were symbolised by Ishtar's followers. They were the vanities, the egoism and the vices of human-beings, and one of them had to stay behind at each gate, until Ishtar passed alone through the last one. Thus she bade farewell to the crown of pride, the cloak of hypocrisy, the sceptre of violence, the necklace of vanity, the veil of selfishness, the girdle of cowardice. Behind the last gate the purified and inspired souls of her entourage welcomed her with a proud and noble dance, in which she joined, no longer ruler but one of them. This play with a "purpose" is an elementary example of how, through the power of the ideas expressed in our dances, I tried to induce my group to relinquish all the enticements of our civilisation. I hardly ever talked about these things, for they were the natural outcome of our way of life on the dance-farm and of the content of our artistic work.

Apart from "Ishtar," we did another fundamental work, a sequence of dances called *The Dancing Drumstick.* This was also a purpose-play, intended to develop by artistic means a sense of rhythm. Somewhere I had come across a book on the meaning of old Mexican drum messages, which gave a wonderful insight into the artistic spiritual character of primitive music, and especially of rhythm. Of course it is impossible to tell the contents in a few words as if they were a story, but I will try to outline some of it, for it may help towards a better understanding of dance. Movement is first and fundamental in what comes forth from a human being as an expression of his intentions and experiences. One must always remember that all sound productions, such as speaking, singing and shouting, spring from physical actions, or in other words from movements. Whether I bang on a table and make it resound, or vibrate the air with shouts, it is always the same thing—movement made audible.

Primitive people have a drum language by which they can communicate with another over unbelievable distances, in a so-to-speak telegraphic manner. Our morse-code apparatus on which an operator taps out a message is by the way also basically nothing other than a refined kind of drum, whose beats are transmitted along an electric cable. The drum-languages of primitive peoples are not phonetic. It is not laid down that, say, one long and one short beat means the letter "A" and another combination of beats any other letter. To primitive man the language of the drum seems nothing other than the rhythm of his body made audible. Therefore, as long as the European tries to investigate it with his intellect it will always remain a mystery to him. Primitive man can make himself understood equally well with audible or with visible gestures. He hears and sees differently from us. The dancer of our cultural era is of course, not a primitive, but he also possesses the same sensitivity to the meaning of visible and audible body movements. For this reason he understands rhythms and sounds as a kind of audible gesture and dance as a visible language.

On my many journeys I marvelled over and over again at how people of all epochs and races had taken infinite pains to build festival arenas, temples and theatres. Worship in ancient times began with festive processions, which were framed by displays illustrating the stories of the gods and heroes of their history. The whole design of the spaces and places for festivity fitted in with the character and form of the sacred act. Every people as well as every epoch has created surroundings in keeping with the highest image of its spiritual aspirations.

The present-day churches of the various creeds and the buildings of the commercial theatres are really nothing but the meagre remnants of a once highly elevated festive culture.

No doubt on the sports fields a coming ideal of man, striving for inner and outer fulfilment, is fostered. Also in the concert halls, which are something new and an invention of our time unknown in earlier civilisations, the breath of the future can sometimes be felt. Today the concert halls are mainly devoted to the encouragement of music, but here and there they are used for performances of artistic dance and dance-plays and these represent a particular and completely new art form.

It became increasingly clear to me that despite the occasional use of the spoken word, my plays, songs and movement pictures did not belong to histrionics or opera but purely to dance. Yet what structure should the place have where dances could be performed and seen as I had dreamed? The problem solved itself, but not through studying or cogitating about it. The solution grew out of my work, it came to me gradually along with the creation and performance of new pieces until in the end I had a picture of the ideal showplace for dance, or rather of various types of showplaces for the various kinds of dance.[6]

But was it really necessary at all to find a frame in the shape of a theatre stage for the kind of performing works I had in mind? Are not groups of moving people, the spoken word and music much more impressive when

---

[6] Laban wrote articles to proclaim the need for places suitable for dancing in and for showing dance. He distinguished between the requirements of the art of stage dance and those of the layman in choric dance and he produced building plans for both. He referred to the former as "dance-theatres" and to the latter as "dance-temples." (*See also* p. 162.)

they speak for themselves? Is there not a danger that all scenery is likely to distract and its colourfulness to divert attention from the essentials which are spoken, danced and acted? My earlier experiences in the traditional theatre strengthened my conviction that we should perform only in the open, or, depending on the weather, in a simple covered hall. Why should we need churches, and theatres with their proscenium arches, stages and scenes? Will not the temple of the future, as well as the stage, be built of the swinging, singing and ringing of human bodies and groups of people? Why this dead and rigid tomb for the arts, this dark vault, in which to imprison that which is divine? We want to glorify life, to see life! And every group of people presenting a work together in concerted action is in itself a living, swinging temple, which fleetingly erects itself and fleetingly disintegrates to make way for new creations. Thus my best-known large-scale *Reigenwerk*, *The Swinging Temple*, came into being. This work demands unusual penetration into the nature of movement, especially in those scenes which have to be danced without musical accompaniment. Most people find it almost impossible at first to dance without an audible stimulus. Only through intense self-awareness can inner and outer inertia be overcome.

It is just as difficult to explain the content of this work as it is to explain the content of pure music. The most one could do would be to describe the play of bodily movements and their patterns in space and for this one would need the help of dance-notation to be even partially successful.

Behind external events the dancer perceives another, entirely different, world. There is an energy behind all occurrences and material things for which it is almost impossible to find a name. A hidden, forgotten landscape lies there, the land of silence, the realm of the soul, and in the centre of this land stands the swinging temple. Yet, the messages from this land of silence are tremendously eloquent and tell us in ever-changing forms and shapes about things and realities important to us all. What we generally call dance also comes from these regions, and the dance-conscious person is truly an inhabitant of this land, consciously and directly drawing strength for living from its inexhaustible treasures. The remaining people can but get a taste of this vital nourishment through the enjoyment they derive from artistic works of dance.

But dance in all its usual forms is certainly not at home in the land of silence. So many of the lamentable prancings and the contrived, hollow gestures, which often pass for dance or as being dance-like, are miles away from that inner attitude out of which true dance arises like a flame and heralds the treasures of our unknown continent. Perception is halfway to possession: perception in the sense that through living fully things are experienced in their wholeness. And it is for this reason that a dancer seeks to experience and not merely to comprehend. Yet a few more words about this strange land. In the jungles and deserts of our planet man can be strangled and devoured by giant snakes and tigers. He can die of thirst or suffocate in the heat; freeze to death in the cold of the north or south, or suffer other disasters. Is it less perilous for travellers in the land of silence? Is it easy to pioneer its exploration? Crossing the borderline may lead to conflict with one's fellows left behind. The keen air which one brings back is only partly accepted. Besides, it is weakening to inhale it only occasionally or in small breaths. Yet even if one does penetrate deeper one can easily lose one's head and fall victim to the strange creatures who inhabit the land.

It would be too much for the reader to grasp if I attempted to describe here the experiences of every excursion into this curious land. Anyone who wants to know more should dance himself, or at least watch true dancing.

But apart from exploring and reporting one can achieve something else, something even more profound. A person can prosper if he settles in that distant land and tills its soil. Its flowers and fruit are works of art woven out of the primeval depths of the inner being. We call them dance, but only truly so if we can identify the threshold of dance, and see the frontier between dance and dance and the gulf that separates the land of silence from our everyday life. To be a peasant in that land, a farmer clearing, ploughing, sowing its fields watching for storms and tempests, struggling against weeds and pests, impatiently waiting for the blessings of harvest, is a life-work just as vigorous, honest and healthy as that of the peasants whose bread we eat. In the heart of the land of silence stands the swinging temple in which all sorrows and joys, all sufferings and dangers, all struggles and deliverances meet and move together. The ever-changing swinging temple, which is built of dances, of dances which are prayers, is the temple of the future.

Despite the success of our summer festivals, our work on the dance-farm was really nothing more than preparatory.[7] Apart from serving our own community we felt increasingly strongly the urge to serve the general public. We had many opportunities during the winter months to go on short tours and give single performances of our works in various towns, but now it became essential to show in a larger setting what we had achieved so far. So with great zest and never disheartened in our efforts we prepared major works and set in motion negotiations for tours and performances. The author of a script for a dance drama called *Victory Through Sacrifice* was enthusiastic about us and saw in our group the perfect instrument for the realisation of his poetry. For this was a work in which the spoken word still played an important part. On the occasion of a great exhibition we were invited to appear with our production in a specially designed theatre.[8] Subsequently, it was decided that an open-air stage and playhouse should be built near a well-known resort in south Germany, with a school for

[7] The previous paragraphs contain reflections made during the ten years following this preparatory period which culminated in the creation of *The Swinging Temple* in 1922.

[8] Hans Brandenburg, the poet and writer, had written a tragedy for the combined expression of dance and word in choric form, called *Der Sieg des Opfers* for Laban to produce. Dr. Konrad Adenauer, Chancellor after World War II, then Burgomaster of Cologne, had invited Laban to perform this work in Cologne at the occasion of the opening of the *Werkbundausstellung* and its new theatre in the Summer of 1914.

dance, sound and the spoken word attached to it.[9] In our group we had several artists who later became well-known,[10] and there was also the young artist who is today considered the greatest dancer in Germany. Her tremendous gift of capturing something of the forces of nature in her dances was brought to a great height through our work together, and we looked forward with pleasure to the effect this would have.[11]

However, our artistic plans were overtaken by the overwhelming events of that time. In our peaceful isolation on the dance-farm we had of course noticed on the political horizon the threatening clouds which were to set our continent on fire. Although I had foreseen long ago that the conflicts between the opposing forces ruling our confused civilisation were causing unbearable tensions which would inevitably erupt into violence, the first declarations of war came as a surprise. I knew the country where the war broke out, and the inflammable situation that had been building up there. But preoccupation with our artistic ideals had thrust everything else into the background. There is a vast difference between the premonition of a catastrophe and being right in the middle of it. It was only natural that our first thoughts would turn to our work which was now in danger, but soon we all realised that much more far-reaching values were at stake. In all the apparently senseless and horrifying events, the readiness to make sacrifices, the enthusiasm and the comradeship became an increasing marvel, almost reconciling one to the madness and even making a kind of sense of it. The only hope was that, after this purging by storm, reason would prevail and that

[9] For considerable time plans had been drawn up for this to be established in Baden-Baden.

[10] Apart from Mary Wigman, Gertrud Leistikow and Suzanne Perrottet, there were among the very mixed crowd of male and female pupils, people such as: Sophie Taeuber, the wife of the famous sculptor Jean Arp, Clair ter Val, the sisters Falke (daughters of the well known North-German poet Gustav Falke), the dancer Laura Oesterreich, Katja Wulff, who later became the director of the Laban school in Basle, and with whom during the year 1916 Laban worked on his plans for a dance-theatre building.

[11] Mary Wigman.

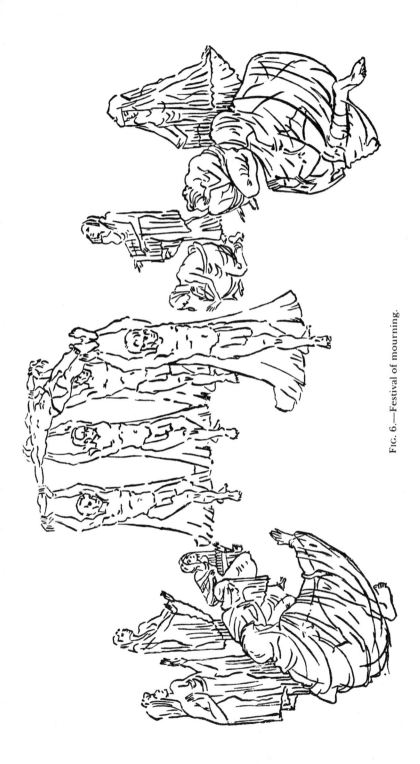

FIG. 6.—Festival of mourning.

instead of the idols and delusions of our artificial civilisation the positive and noble instincts of human nature
would regain the upper hand. But we were still a long
way from that.

Not only did the destruction of my instrument and the
end of all hopes and endeavours have to be overcome,
but it also gave me time to reflect, and from this came a
new inner adaptation to the artistic tasks of dance. In my
youth I had lived only for the works that came from
concern with my own experiences, but I now recognised
my responsibility towards the young people in my care,
towards the community of dancers which was to become
my instrument. Now it was clear too, that over and above
this there was also an obligation and responsibility
towards the larger community of all those whom my art
could be expected to serve. These many people are not
just customers and buyers, nor are we artists just egocen-
tric producers who are allowed to dream our dreams in
isolation. We are all one, and what is at stake is the
universal soul out of which and for which we have to
create. Such a realisation does not bear fruit overnight.
Our endeavours towards this goal and the way we paved
only became visible as our art developed.

Chapter 2

ILLUSIONS

DAZZLED by the vision of the inner life I tried to shape tangible characters from the forces at work within man. The conflict between the subconscious mind of the individual and that of the masses became the content of my new dance-plays. The fluttering of these characters, lighting up and dimming down, dazzled me like bright will-o'-the-wisps at night. The spectacle of the dark regions of inner forces, of the play of energies which shape our lives so potently, was for me just as alive as the representation of external nature. To this period belongs our first theatrical dance-play on a somewhat larger scale: *The Deluded.*[1] The main trend of this play is not difficult to describe. Individual beings who are friends with each other join to form a glittering but deceptive unity. A multi-armed idol comes into being, who, however, keeps disintegrating into his separate components of violent, servile, dreaming, searching, raving, paralysing forces.

[1] Original title in German, *Die Geblendeten*. This was created in 1921 at the Mannheim National Theatre where Laban was engaged as Ballet master. It was first performed there with a group of forty dancers half of whom were Laban's own group and the other half the permanent Ballet company of the theatre—a tremendous undertaking to bring dancers with such different outlooks on dance to a common movement expression. Repeat performances were soon afterwards given, in January 1922, at the Württembergische Landestheater in Stuttgart. During the years 1920–22 Laban resided in Stuttgart where he trained twenty-five pupils as a performing group Among them were Kurt Jooss, Jens Keith, Edgar Frank, Herta Feist and Albrecht Knust. Laban drew on this group during his engagement in the Mannheim theatre which he attended from his Stuttgart residence.

Eventually, though, the diverging tendencies are united in an organised dance in which through the affinity between the characters, before unnoticed and unrecognised, a true togetherness becomes possible. In this play I avoided giving names such as king, beggar, priest and nun to the inner forces appearing in it. It was performed almost silently, without music, without explanation, without a list of characters—simply as pure dance. I was amazed by the tremendous impact it had on everyone who saw it. The language of dance had undoubtedly been understood.

In my longest and best-known dramatic dance-work, the dance-ballad *Illusions*,[2] I gave names to the forces and let their play take its course within a given frame of action.

The basic idea behind *Illusions* is a social experience. An individual, who rises to power over a community, all too easily becomes a slave to his own might. In the same way, rebels who rise up against authority are rarely capable of becoming true leaders. They mostly succumb to cynical pessimism when personal experience and the defects inherent in their environment either arouse their suspicions or depress them. In the end, they lose faith in their own ideals and condemn their achievements as useless and vain. From this springs hatred of people which leads to tyranny. The whole of life becomes an illusion—and so the dance-ballad got its name.

It begins with a happily dancing group of country-folk suddenly interrupted by the appearance of a tyrannic character. The dancing peasants hide themselves and even the idling attendants of the tyrant freeze with fear. A beggar, the symbol of inner need, is chased away with kicks in answer to his laments. Not even the court jester with his capers can ease the tension. A dancing juggler, who tries to amuse and enliven the people with his art, rouses the wrath of the tyrant. His anger turns into

[2] This is an attempt to capture the approximate meaning of the German title *Die Gaukelei*, literally translated as "Jugglery." Laban first produced this work with his professional company, *Tanzbühne Laban*, in Hamburg in 1923.

senseless fury, when the juggler puts the princess, symbol of longing for happiness and beauty, so strongly under his spell that she joins in the dance and raises herself into a state of dreamlike bliss. In the end, the fury of the tyrant leads to the chaining of the juggler and the exile of the princess, who, now one of the disinherited, joins the beggar.

The juggler is led away, everybody flees, and the tyrant remains behind alone stiff and motionless. Then the beggar and the princess can be seen in feverish flight. The people want to wrest the princess—the longing for happiness—from the beggar, the bearer of need; but he hides her.

The hangman, representing the will of the tyrant, enters to execute the dancing juggler, inciter of desire. The beggar goads the people on to resist, the execution is prevented, and as the people wrench the axe away from the executioner, the juggler escapes. But the tyrant has the people punished and whipped, and in their humiliation they take revenge on the instigator, the beggar, and strangle him. His body is finally found by thoughtful court-jesters, the murderers having quietly sneaked away one by one.

Into a circle of dark figures steps the juggler, his playful dancing over. He wants to summon the figures to a solemn dance, to turn them into a machine, into a stream of energy to help him destroy the tyranny of hate. He wants to replace this paralysing violence with his cheerful play and so bring lasting happiness to the people.

The tyrant meets the juggler amidst the conspirators and, tremendously agitated, he confronts him. He commands the conspirators to arrest him, but these dark figures are under the spell of the juggler's promises and turn away from the tyrant. Seeing himself abandoned and judged by everyone he collapses and dies. The symbol of hate is destroyed.

The princess, defenceless through the death of the beggar, runs for protection to the juggler who receives her with gladness. But then she sees the body of the tyrant and in despair she breaks away from the juggler, believing him to be the murderer. Doubt that serene grace and peaceful happiness are ever possible drives her into madness and she flees.

When the juggler tries to follow her, the conspirators hold him back. He no longer belongs to himself but to them all. Solemnly they drape the tyrant's cloak over his shoulders, for he is to be their ruler.

Mourning women tell the juggler of the princess' death. Her rigid body is carried past high on upstretched arms. He cannot follow her over the threshold which she has crossed. When the people come to acclaim him he pulls himself together, but stands benumbed amid the joys of the festivity.

Soon a serious, embittered man sits on the throne once again, and even when he tries to cheer himself up the dances around him become as sombre and weird as he is. His passionate searching appears so grotesque that all his people finally forsake him. The juggler realises that rigidity and death are the end of all things. Before his eyes there appears a gruesome dance in slow motion by the three dead characters, the beggar, the tyrant and the princess. Need and hate are dead but so is longing. He feels the tyrant wresting the crown and cloak of power from him, leaving him as he was before, a poor juggler, but he can say nothing to the insensible dead.

Suddenly, his image leaps in, teasing him with his own former capers. His double shows him the trifling play of his youthful longings. The juggler wants to catch the image, to look into his eyes, to unravel the enigmas of his own life. Gropingly, he tries to approach the reflection. Slowly their hands meet. At that moment, the other self vanishes and the juggler collapses. The three figures of the dead fall upon him, and together they shrink into a shapeless heap.

The jester enters, and the endlessly repetitive play of human longing for happiness is over once again. But the people, representing everlasting strength, dance on, disregarding the struggles and sufferings of the individual.

Years had passed by, along the banks of Lake P.,[3] every hundred paces or so, there are lonely little cottages with colourful gardens. There we had taken up our quarters and split up into groups with three or four or even more to a house. We could not find a covered hall for our rehearsals anywhere in the neighbourhood so instead we used a big meadow near the lake. After practices we would go for a swim and then back to work again, but this only continued for the few sunny weeks we had. Then it began to rain and rain for weeks and months. There were some dry half days but it was very cool. We practised in small groups of five to seven in the halls of nearby village inns. Each group had assigned tasks, exercises and dances and the work was supervised by one of them as leader. Every day I went on my round from one village to another several times and felt just like a country postman, my big cloak hardly ever getting dry. In the various inns I sometimes found that I did not only have to contend with art: very often I had to straighten things out with landlords and landladies who were not as pleased with the hustle and bustle as one might have expected from good business people. Year in year out they had been used to relaxing and dozing on weekdays in order to recover from the rather livelier Sundays. But now it was Sunday and dance every day! And what a dance! Although their guests seemed harmless and friendly enough, they had some rather peculiar ways at times. One landlady maintained that so much dancing had made her chickens rebellious and that they had

[3] Here Laban picks up the thread from the end of the last chapter where he recalled the time of the outbreak of World War I, in the Autumn of 1914. Now, he is in Gleschendorf near the lake of Pönitz in Holstein in the summer of 1922. Laban's circle had grown to more than forty members. People like *Sylvia Bodmer*, who later was the co-director with Lotte Müller of the Laban school in Frankfurt and who has been teaching in Manchester, England since 1940; *Ruth Loeser* who became Laban's partner in his many "pure" dance recital programmes; *Julian Algo*, later Ballet master and director of dance in Scandinavia; *Dido Larasse* who became known in England as lecturer and writer on dance under his real name of Dr. Landes; *Lotte Wedekind*, the niece of the poet Frank Wedekind, later the director of one of the Laban schools in Berlin and Lisa Ullmann's teacher, *Aino Siimola*, later Kurt Jooss' wife and rehearsal assistant, joined the others.

stopped laying. I had a nasty suspicion that some of my youngsters had pinched the eggs, but this could not be proved. At any rate, I forbade them to enter the barns and stables during rest-periods. In another village inn a group had used table-linen and freshly-laundered curtains for costume studies and performances of veildances. A third landlord had yet another complaint, and it was not easy to pacify these people. One autumn evening, returning from my rounds at dusk, I noticed some strange large birds sitting in the tree-tops of an orchard. They did not stir. As I drew nearer I had a suspicion that they were one of my dance-groups, out on a fruit-raid. I always wondered at these young people who, having grown up in war-time, had lost all respect for property. After getting them down and giving them a piece of my mind there was an imposition of extra training in the damp meadows. Then we assessed the amount of fruit eaten and reimbursed the owner for a good hundredweight.

On many of my lonely walks over the bleak rain-drenched countryside I kept on thinking how to give stability and form to my pupils' youthful enthusiasm for movement. I remembered the works I had dreamed of many years ago, and my thoughts finally settled on *The Swinging Temple*, which I resolved to perform. Indeed, it was high time to gather the unruly groups together in one common task. I found a fairly large hall and in a few weeks we created our first large-scale *Reigenwerk*. It was a work of five *Reigen*, lasting altogether three hours. Some parts had no musical accompaniment at all and were to be danced in silence—in the land of silence; others had percussion accompaniment. Most of the dances were, however, conceived with a melodic and harmonic background. The music arose simultaneously with the dances, which I reconstructed from memory as my former sketches had got lost. Our young conductor became one of the best-known composers for dance in later years.[4]

[4] Friedrich Wilckens who later became a close associate of Harold Kreuzberg, the world-famous male dance soloist, as his music composer and accompanist. Wilckens had worked with Laban already in Stuttgart and Mannheim. (*See also* p. 109.)

In each *Reigen* of *The Swinging Temple* a different
dance-temperament was represented. It was almost a
history of the art of dance. From primordial rhythmic
movement-impulses to the controlled and polylinear
structure of priestly stepping, all forms of human aspirations for dance were represented. Magical and ecstatic
dances alternated with comic and combative scenes.
When I later performed this work I was advised to have a
first-aid party with stretchers in readiness as it was
thought that nobody would survive three hours of dance,
especially dance of such healthy and natural vigour as
ours, which had grown out of the country life we had
been leading. The whole composition was very lively and
impressive.

But the pessimists were wrong. *The Swinging Temple*
became one of our biggest successes with both the public
and the press. Never before or after did I receive such
tremendous ovations as at performances of this work. It
was obvious that we had achieved a completely new style,
indeed a new way of working in the field of the performing arts. It was called a movement-symphony, a name I
did not care for because a symphony is a purely musical
expression. Quite rightly, nobody called it a drama. Yet
no name could be found for this oratorio-like form of the
art of dance, and even today there is no universally-
accepted name for it, although its style was widely
approved and copied. Subsequently I created many
other such works. Now for the first time my movement-
dreams which decades ago had inspired me when working on *The Earth*, were to some extent fulfilled. At first I
was even undecided if I should produce *The Earth*. But
The Earth and *The Night* alike were conceived primarily
as cantatas with the group dances as a kind of visual
complement and I rather wanted to produce a pure
dance-work which was, so to speak, for vision alone. The
idea was to become immediately clear from the movements, and for this *The Swinging Temple* was very suitable. We had also prepared a few smaller, humorous items
which I hoped we could perform somewhere, in spite of
our troubled times.

We ate our meals in a large barn. The mother of one of
my most faithful pupils made delicious soups from

potatoes and vegetables which were very difficult to obtain and at a price we could hardly afford.[5] Now and then we were able to get a small piece of bacon or meat. In the evenings, the barn served as our assembly-room, and there, by the scant light of stable-lanterns, we discussed the profoundest problems of the art of dancing and community life. We also had festivities both for ourselves and for the local people and eventually we even had visitors from neighbouring towns coming to inspect this "fool's paradise." Some of these visitors soon became true admirers of our art and later generous supporters. From this developed our first independent dance-theatre which I shall discuss later on.[6] Until then we had to survive a long and difficult time. Meanwhile we gave several recitals in the surrounding villages partly to practise performing and partly to earn some money. In the inns where we had previously rehearsed we were received either with enthusiastic encouragement or with fierce rejection, which several times threatened to develop into dangerous fights. The return home at night was never free from the worry that one of the dancers, bowled over by success, might disappear into the lake. They were not all such good swimmers that one could anticipate such an incident calmly. But when the morning roll-call came they all were present and our work ripened that autumn, emulating the tempting fruit on the trees.

Then it grew cold. Our rooms were mostly unheatable. Anyway, we had not intended staying for ever. In fact, we had originally planned to go our separate ways in the autumn and had only come together for joint practice. But the bond between us had become so strong and the enthusiasm for the work, which had grown out of our living together, also contributed to making a separation,

---

[5] The post-war years and inflation had brought extreme privations to everyone. Through the help of Albrecht Knust's mother, who concocted some kind of dishes from whatever could be had, the group had at least one regular daily meal.

[6] The *Tanzbühne Laban*, the professional dance-theatre company. They prepared programmes for performances in the coming season.

at that stage, out of the question. They all declared that they would go with me through thick and thin. This was as it should be, because our group had grown out of nothing and its continuation could only be achieved by conscientious perseverance.

So first transforming myself into a manager with the purchase of a beautiful overcoat and cap which were duly admired, I set out. My last pennies were just sufficient to pay for a railway ticket to the nearest large sea-port,[7] where, through introductions from one of the enthusiastic visitors to our country festivities, I got to know people who were to become good, or even best, friends of myself and of our art. They lent me a hand and at last I found my way to influential people who were in a position to support our work. I outlined our artistic endeavours as well as I could, for no prospectus, no photographs, and none of the usual publicity material were available. A manager of a theatre[8] gave me a contract on the spot for fourteen late-night performances, and payment in advance enabled my group to travel. However, the housing shortage was so great that I became a laughing stock over my attempts to find lodgings for my fifty members. "You won't even get hold of ten beds!" I was told, "unless you're as rich as Croesus and can book into the best hotels." Again I managed to speak so convincingly to some influential people of the value and beauty of our endeavours that in the end even a clergyman in his Sunday sermon succeeded in getting his parishioners to put up our young women-dancers. After much trouble and difficulty the fifty beds became available at reasonable prices, and I could go to fetch my group.

Back at Lake P. I was awaited with suspense. It was pouring with rain, and the poor devils were shivering with cold and despondency. My report was received with shouts of joy, followed by a rush for home to pack, and soon our strange caravan was on the way to the station.

[7] Hamburg.

[8] The *Deutsche Bühnen*, later called *Hamburger Bühnen*, sponsored Laban and under their aegis a number of his theatrical as well as choric dance works were performed.

My assistant was a dancer who had witnessed our time on the dance-farm.[9] She was the only one left of this earlier large group. Some had gone their own ways, a few of the boys had been killed in the war and of several others we had completely lost sight. Only this dancer was still with me from the dance-farm days and completely involved with my work. The style of her movements was inspired, and her strong gift as an art-educator made her particularly suitable to help me with the tasks I had set myself. To a great extent I owed to her the development of the new group. Besides assisting me with the training of the company, she also danced the leading parts in our compositions. Yet the latter were all group works and the leading parts were not in any sense star or glamorous roles. Strictly speaking, they only carried greater responsibility.

Our late-night performances served their purpose. They kept our heads above water for a start. We performed a few of my earlier dance-plays. Some of it was almost too heavy a fare for our audiences. But the dancing was so lively that they took pleasure in watching the fresh and beautiful movements of these young people even if they did not understand much about our art.

There was no great difficulty in finding new contacts, but to get reasonable contracts, which would bring us even halfway to realising our serious artistic aims, seemed out of the question at first. We had to fight for everything with our last ounce of energy. It was a miracle how we scraped through alive. Amidst continuing unrest and uncertainty and even climbing over barricades we sought work and bread.[10] My famous cloak got more holes each time I set out to obtain food supplies for our hungry young women. At times we had to use our fists in defence of our humane and artistic principles, as moral deterioration, particularly in our sphere of work, became

---

[9] Dussia Bereska. She had joined Laban's circle in Switzerland in 1916 and worked with him up to the 1930s.

[10] In 1923 there was the communist uprising in Hamburg. Also, inflation in Germany reached its climax during that year.

alarmingly evident. We had no permanent home which could have provided some protection and I, as father of this large family, had my hands full in coping with the most urgent everyday needs. At last we met people who recognised the sincerity of our artistic endeavours and who helped us to get suitable engagements.

We designed and made our own costumes, rehearsed the musical accompaniment with members of our group, decorated the halls and as far as possible produced everything ourselves. This was not only done for economy's sake but also because of our artistic convictions, and it contributed enormously to the striking unity of our productions. Even the smallest detail of the scenery, every operation, every note, every step and all the necessary arrangements were animated by our collective artistic determination. I often looked back on these times later when I suffered from the inner emptiness and insipid superficiality of the extravagant and lavish performances which were staged in big theatres and in which I was compelled to participate. I have already mentioned that the first performance of *The Swinging Temple* was a tremendous success, which nearly made us forget the wild turmoil of those times. In any event, this dance-work brought us the possibility, much-dreamt-of though hardly expected, of having our own four walls in which to establish a permanent dance-theatre.

One must not suppose that this cultural deed came about through love of dance alone. We were still a long way from that! It was a fortunate circumstance for us that the zoological gardens of the town[11] where we had settled had got into financial difficulties. The wonderful monkeys, zebras and elephants led their contemplative lives in a deserted garden. Nobody wanted to look at the animals. The festival halls of the main building were equally deserted, and for no obvious reason the inhabitants celebrated their weddings and social gatherings somewhere else.

[11] Hamburg Zoological Gardens had extensive halls for banquets, exhibitions, concerts and such like.

"We must get the people used to the zoo again" said one of the principal shareholders, and so it was natural that he would think of bringing in any kind of wild-life show as a means of attraction. But as it happened there were no Wild-West riders or cannibal-dancers in the offing and so the next grand idea was to put these festival rooms at our disposal in the secret hope that during the summer months we would give performances on a lawn next to the monkey-house. I found it extremely difficult to keep a straight face during the preliminary discussions, or to swallow my indignation, but I had an idea and fifty children to care for. The main thing, I said to myself, is what one makes of an opportunity and not how it is offered. I made a contract with the zoo management and asked for a hall to be adapted as a theatre, and this was carried out precisely according to my specifications.

A considerable number of subscribers came to visit our regular performances. Without further explanation, it is difficult to convey how much it meant to us to be able to operate our own floodlights and to ring our own curtain up and down. Ours was the first and the only specialised dance-theatre, the first and probably also the last in Europe for some time to come, for we have travelling dance-groups but no resident dance-theatres. It was left to our chamber-dance-group to make this bold beginning. The idea of founding a chamber-dance theatre and giving it this particular name came from my brave and inspired colleague, the one who had helped with the organisation and training of the group.[12] A wealth of delightful short dance-works were produced with her both participating and directing. Later, the support of an arts association enabled us to produce dance-works for large groups in an exhibition hall next door to the chamber-dance theatre. At that time we still included the spoken word in our dance. I used in particular speech

---

[12] In 1924 the *Kammertanzbühne Laban*—chamber-dance group—was founded with Dussia Bereska as director. This was a small group of three to seven dancers which had a different function from that of the *Tanzbühne Laban*, the large performing company, or the *Hamburger Movement Choirs Laban* under the leadership of Albrecht Knust.

choirs,[13] but single speakers also took part, as for example in *Prometheus*, an old Greek drama, which I extended
with movement-choir scenes for prologues, entr'actes
and epilogues. We even ventured to produce Goethe's
Faust, that is to say, the second part. Our denigrators
talked about "dance impudence," but where would we be
if we never wanted to be impudent! We also performed
other works of the pure dance kind, and what we did set
the standard for later dance productions in Germany.
Besides silent dances we performed works to the accompaniment of gong, drum and flute, or to simple music.
All our music was composed expressly for our dances;
existing music was really only used for folk dance.

Dance always came first. Directly out of our work and
without deliberate planning we invented new and typical
kinds of dance which I could not however analyse so
clearly then as I can today. When I read the old titles on
the programmes of those days and recall the dances, I
realise what an important role the source of dance
invention has. The dances *Joy-grief*, *Shadows*, *Dreams* and
many others convey even through their titles that they
are representations of inner stirrings. At other times, a
feeling for form, a delight in line was predominant, or
invention came from a more pictorial imagination. To
these belong the dance *The Crystal*, which divided space
on hard, severe lines, the dance *Arabesques* and also a solo
by our leading dancer which became well-known and
which was almost a symbol of the spirit of our theatre. It
was called *The Orchid*, a composition of the most subtle
arm and finger movements which got its name because it
seemed to express the inner life of a bizarre flower in the
process of unfolding, *The Magic Garden*, a similar work
but for a small group, was also born out of the pictorial
imagination. I am not listing these titles without reason,
but because all these dances were somehow foreshadowed in my songs of *The Earth*. One of my solo
dances, *Caprice*, and also the group play *The Cranks' Club*,

---

[13] A more detailed description of the choric works, including *Faust* and
Prometheus, can be found on p. 160.

which later formed a basis for our dance suite *The Green Clowns*, were reminiscent of the images of *The Night*. So was *Homunculus*, the artificial man, *The Robot* and numerous other dances which we presented under the title *Fantastic Show*. They were mime dances, characterising city experiences. So country and town, nature and civilisation all motivated and inspired us to give form to our inner visions.

Therefore, familiar characters came into being, who were welcomed by the audience like old acquaintances just as in the medieval theatre. There were, for example, the jester, the juggler, obstinacy, rage, playfulness, the dandy, the tyrant, death and many others. Female roles are usually not so clearly defined; a woman is inwardly more flexible and yet more unified.

The fact that traditional and especially national and folk dances, which I had known since my youth, were actively cultivated by us goes without saying. But we also sought out and found new variations of the basic forms of German, Hungarian, Slav, Romanic, English and other exotic dances. In our choice of decor and costume we still wavered between a stylisation of historical and theatrical forms on the one hand, and the new characteristic style of our simple dance dress on the other. We even performed the same dances in different costumes, sometimes in a historical and at others in a timeless way so that we would not simply be guided by our own taste but also by reactions of the audiences, whom after all we wanted to attract in the first place.

Of the more important chamber-dance plays I want to mention *The Dragon Slayer*, a fairy-tale dance which later was made into one of the first sound films.[14] We sometimes tried incorporating very simple movements and even everyday gestures into our dances. Some plays were built up out of affirmative nods, negative shakings of the head, defensive movements of the hands, beckoning waves, arms opening in surprise and similar everyday

[14] This was in Berlin in 1927. Lisa Ullmann witnessed the rigours of the first sound film experiments, as Laban had asked her to dance one of the "lilies" in the magic garden scene.

movements. The result of such experiments was both fascinating and stimulating. An audience will only be attracted to attend a dance-theatre regularly and maintain its interest if there is diversity in what is offered—something we possessed at that happy and fruitful time—and also if the particular types of dance are carefully articulated and arranged. Only in this way is it possible to gain new friends for the art of dance and to increase understanding of it. Obviously, there has to be meaning and substance behind everything. Pure play with forms is by no means art yet. We were undoubtedly pioneers in the organisation of programmes for the dance-theatre and till the last days of its existence our theatre was booked up and very popular. But at a time of general economic depression it was impossible for an enterprise like ours which was only in its infancy to keep going any longer.[15]

A tragicomic pantomime *Above and Below*,[16] later called *Star Gazer*, was often performed, and not only had a strong appeal for audiences but was also appreciated by the press. It opened with a divided stage showing the starlit sky above and the star gazers below. With meticulous angular movements they execute their measurings and observations. Their wives enter and want to take them away from their work. The three scholars, however, continue to wait unflinchingly for new stars, forgetting the world around them and their evening meal. A merry crowd passes by and carries off the women. The astronomers stay behind, and their patience is rewarded, for on the upper stage appear the evening star and two comets followed by many other stars and eventually by the moon in person.

We composed the music at the same time as the dances and suddenly one day, during a rehearsal, the musical

[15] Towards the end of 1924 the large company—*Tanzbühne Laban*—had to be abandoned and all theatrical production work was then concentrated in the *Kammertanzbühne* which carried on for many more years.

[16] This work was first performed in Stuttgart in 1922 with Bereska, Jooss and Knust as protagonists. Friedrich Wilckens composed the music for it. A drawing by Laban of the stargazer is included in this book on p. 4.

motif for the moon was born. Our leading lady who performed the moon was dancing with such elan and expression that all the members of the cast spontaneously hummed and whistled a melody which became the accompaniment. For years the moon motif remained our signature tune, which we used for calling and communicating with one another.

One day, walking along the beach of the Pacific Ocean near San Francisco and thinking myself far away from everyone I knew, I suddenly heard the moon motif being whistled. I followed the sound. To my greatest surprise and joy I soon stood face to face with a dear old colleague who had not expected in the least to meet me here. We talked about our *Star gazer* play.

"Do you remember how the astronomers tried to clamber up towards the stars only to fall down again?"

"And how delightful and unapproachably cool the heavenly bodies were as they danced their undeviating rounds."

"Were you dancing with the merry crowd of women and soldiers?"

"And wasn't it gorgeous how the impudent X jumped on the upper stage and how he declared his love to the comet!"

"Yes, and what happened then?"

"Well, don't you remember, the impudent X lured the comet down to the earth-people whereupon the evening star jumped angrily on to the earth to punish the impertinent mortals. Then a battle arose in which the moon intervened as peacemaker and the stars and people celebrated with a festival, and the moon finally led the merry party into the heavens."

We had to laugh at the memory of the pensive astronomers and their consternation over the irregular behaviour of the heavenly bodies. One of them, however, suspected the presence of another heaven and climbed with difficulty on to the upper stage. But he was too late, and plunged grotesquely into nothingness.

So once more on this other side of the globe we happily whistled our moon motif.

Of our theatrical dance-plays, *The Comedy*,[17] which was about Casanova and his tragicomical experiences, was particularly popular. This work was convincing theatre in great style. I danced the philosophically-inspired servant and companion of the big-mouthed Casanova, match-making and even procuring Venus and her three graces for him. The servant had of course to fight all his master's battles, and to go through all sorts of unsavoury adventures with the devil who was after Casanova's soul. My old friends Kasperl and "Napoleum" doubtless stood godfathers in this.

Then, led astray by external success, I unfortunately overstepped the frontiers of my art. I got out a burlesque Revue which, though received with loud acclamation, lost me many friends.[18] Properly considered, it was a serious enough work; it was an obvious mockery of audiences which only have a taste for slight entertainment.

Now I have drawn many laughs in my time. In Paris, for instance, a woman in the audience got into such hysterics over one of my favourite jests in the dance *Caprice* mentioned earlier, that she had to be taken away by a rescue squad. But never before or since have I ever had such a laughter success as with this Revue. The auditorium resounded with roars and in the front stalls I saw the most serious personages doubled up. I had to lower the curtain myself, as the attendant was put out of action by fits of laughter. It is not good, however, to make people laugh too much; they may forgive you less readily for this than for an emotional response which has to be wrung out of them. It seems that in this world being serious has the most aristocratic air. I hoped that a successful run of one of our particular attractions would save my theatre, but it fell victim to the time of trial in which we lived. The laundry baskets full of inflated

[17] First shown in Hamburg in 1923.

[18] This performance took place in the *Hamburger Schauspielhaus* in November 1924. It was strongly rejected by many of the press, while others wrote that it is "representative of Laban's highest and most mature art."

Fig. 7.—The tyrant and his victim.

paper-money which our performances earned were in the end hardly sufficient to buy a loaf of bread. In those days, the authorities showed not the slightest understanding of our endeavours. "Why should there be a dance-theatre? Germans have no use for dance," was always the answer when I tried to expound my ideas to influential people. Yet, I had, and still have, massive evidence of how greatly the German public long for dance and enjoy dance of every kind.

In order to secure a livelihood we had no alternative but to go on tour which also took us abroad several times.[19] It was good that in this way we could test out the general validity of our work in the wider world.

[19] The *Tanzbühne Laban* toured throughout Germany, giving performances in most major cities. In the spring and summer of 1924 they toured in Austria, Italy and extensively in Yugoslavia.

Chapter 3

THE TITAN

ON my travels I saw dances of many peoples of the world
and experienced over and over again the power of
community-dancing. This found expression in my big-
gish *Reigenwerk The Titan* and below I have put down
excerpts from my travel-diary, which give an idea of the
impressions which influenced this work.[1]

Arrival in U.S.A.

In a force ten gale, more than eleven days rolling on
the ocean in fog and between icebergs in a comparatively
small boat. American zeal equal to windforce ten. I
wonder which of the two are more dangerous and
terrifying: the angry elements or the crazy high tension
of over-excited human brains. In the same way that one
gets used to the rolling of the oceans, so one gets used to
the mechanism of the U.S.A. In Europe, my plans hardly
attract attention any more; here they evidently want to
build golden bridges for me. Reporters boarded the ship
together with the customs officers. It did not enter my
mind that these gentlemen had any notion of my humble
existence. I was even more amazed when suddenly a man
with a straw hat pushed to the back of his head and a pipe
in his mouth, performed some wild tap dancing in front
of me on the unsteady deck. He asked me abruptly "Can

[1] In May 1926 Laban travelled to North America for the purpose of
ethnographical studies. His journey was interrupted by the death of his
mother in Geneva in October 1926 when he had to return to Europe.

you write this down?" He had obviously heard of my dance notation. Then he took one hand out of his trouser-pocket and offered me his sleeve on which to write down his tappings. I asked him to repeat them, which he did, and then I scribbled a few dance notation signs on his cuff. Soon he was joined by a few more gentlemen who resembled him to a T. One of them asked me if a person's soul could be expressed in a "Salto Mortale"—that is a somersault in the air—and if I would demonstrate it. Another was anxious to learn how many thousands of dollars I would charge for producing a dance. Next day there appeared in the newspaper full-page articles with headlines such as "Master of Dance declares the charleston as the crown of all dances." (We had not discussed the charleston at all.) "German Dancer and woman partner are going to perform three salto mortales as religious exercise." (Rather exaggerated!) "A Gentleman who can tell your character from your slightest movement."(Result of a talk on a dancer's temperament.) "A new way to success. Mr. L. teaches how to write down dances. You can earn millions with this." (He was referring to my dance notation.) Underneath were photographs of people quite unknown to me in contorted positions, and described as my only, true and most successful pupils. The following day, a man came to see me and produced an already completed contract which, in return for a fabulous salary and my own offices in a skyscraper on Broadway, bound me for five years to make up correspondence courses on the charleston and similar dances, and distribute them all over the world. At the same time another applicant stormed into my room proposing that by next Thursday I should choreograph for a Broadway theatre four large group ballets with myself as Premier Danseur. (I shall keep these contracts as mementos.) Considering that nobody in Europe has troubled about my dance notation it is astonishing how these people have a nose for the novel features in my work. It is obvious that they are out for gain; however, all these estimable offers are out of the question for me. There must be other ways of getting to know America.

For me the most fascinating thing in a country which has all races on board is to make comparative dance studies. I haven't the least intention of carrying on with my ideas here. The spirit of the robot is far too strong for this. I don't want anything to do with money-making for its own sake, for it is simply a waste of time.

California

It seems as if a new variation of the white race is about to develop in California. Travelling south from Los Angeles towards the Mexican border, one comes across strange kinds of holiday centres where people's cultural hankerings are quite different from anywhere else in the world. If one is not put off by the fact that they are in reality hotels for multi-millionaires, one can become acquainted with all sorts of stirrings of the human soul. We were touring in that direction when the car got stuck in the sand in an apparently endless desert and it was only with great difficulty that we extricated ourselves. These paradises are situated in oases and one can only reach them via a desert. An acquaintance of mine, the technical director of a Hollywood film company, drew my attention to one particularly remarkable hotel. "You simply must go and see it, it's better than the cleverest film—there's every kind of style on earth, luxury beyond words, crazy customs, and so on." But to me it did not seem so crazy. As I said, I even thought that here were beginnings of a new cultural endeavour.

Having arrived[2] and parked the car in an outer courtyard, we were guided through several tastefully and comfortably furnished lounges. All around, useful objects were informally arranged. Everything, including the pictures on the walls, had obvious artistic value. Stress on period styles was avoided. Through a second court-yard we came in to the real entrance hall of the hotel but no notices or advertisements were to be seen. Here again we felt as though we were in the hall of a country mansion rather than on business premises. It was discreetly made

[2] This was at the Mission Inn near Los Angeles.

clear that guests were not to be troubled with bills, dirty
paper-money and suchlike, and we were therefore,
requested to pay in advance a certain sum, quite modest
in fact, which would entitle us to make use of all the
facilities as we pleased. Once again we had to cross a
smallish courtyard, at the entrance of which there were
two huge church bells. One was Chinese and the other
Christian, dating from the Franciscan missions which, as
is well-known, had come along the coast from San
Francisco and were the first white colonists to spread
European beliefs. Just at that moment chimes of bells
rang out from the rooftops and we heard them again
later at fifteen-minute intervals. The sound was novel
and strange but entirely harmonious. Lining the inner
court were loggia-like rooms, and all round the upper
stories were balconies reminding us that we were in a
country with a strong Spanish influence. On several
terraces there were tables and chairs, not arranged in
ranks but in a most unconventional and imaginative way;
wonderful plants, too, and a few tall palm trees reaching
far above the roofs of the surrounding buildings. From a
bamboo grove came sounds of guitars and other plucked
instruments, somehow resembling a far-off twittering of
birds, and blending pleasantly with the faint murmur of
a delicate fountain. Most curious were the little bells and
images of gods of various shapes and origin which were
attached to the uneven roof edges of the surrounding
buildings. They produced a finely-tuned play of chimes,
each note coming from a different direction, which made
the melodies even more fascinating. Between the tables
nimble Indios flitted in white-stockinged feet: they are
people of small stature, a mixed race of Japanese and
Red Indian. A race eager to serve, their subordination
inborn. Later on, I learnt that apparently only white,
healthy and well-built people were allowed in through
the inconspicuously controlled entrances. In any case,
there were no worldly women and the men behaved with
pleasant restraint. Yet one felt free. Suddenly, as if by
magic, the table was elegantly laid in front of us with
minute portions of a peculiar combination of choice

dishes. As soon as they had been tasted, they were exchanged for others and it seemed that the order of succession was intended to give the palate a certain harmonious experience. The stuff was delicious, but with such small portions overeating was impossible no matter how hard one tried.

Between two of the quarter-hourly chimes the enchanting voice of a woman rang out, unobtrusively singing some short songs. Afterwards, one could stroll through the rooms, or sit down; valuable books were lying around, but I saw no newspapers or magazines. On one side there was a swimming pool of blue glass with silvery edges. Flowers were everywhere and their scents gave the impression of being somehow carefully chosen to blend with the colours and shapes of the rooms. "This can't be the whole story," I said to my friends, "it is surely the most aesthetic hotel in the world, but there must be something else behind it all." My friends wanted to relax a little longer in the beautiful surroundings and left it to me to go alone on a reconnaisance.

By chance I found on one of the shelves a European book on dance which included some pictures of my performances. I took it out, went to the reception hall and asked to speak to the manager. I introduced myself to him and told him that I had come to the States to study and would very much like to see the rest of his amazing hotel. My credentials were easily proved by means of the book held in my hand. He seemed genuinely pleased to make my acquaintance and said he had already come across my name somewhere, which was not impossible, of course, considering the garish publicity the New York press had given me. He asked what language I preferred to converse in as he wanted to put a guide at my disposal immediately. That was how I met Miss F., a young woman of great charm and wit. Although in my profession I have plenty of opportunity to meet beautiful and intelligent women from all walks of life and different countries, Miss F. surprised me by the combination of natural vivacity and broad education which she evinced during our tour of inspection. With my inclination to imagine spirits it is not surprising that I soon counted this young lady among the angelic creatures which one unfortunately meets so rarely.

She took me to a different part of the extensive complex of buildings and we entered a very large, lofty room with some hundred armchairs standing about. These chairs looked as if they had been collected from all over the world. Exotic golden thrones stood next to massive German and stiff French antique armchairs. Carved benches, Indian sofas, Chinese Mandarin-seats and all kinds of other valuable armchairs mingled in colourful confusion, their casualness presenting a beautiful overall picture. By a narrow wall there was an elevated area with a heavy, broad table in front of a large coloured glass window. Nearby to the right and to the left, organpipes gleamed in the semi-darkness.

"This is our assembly-room," explained the angel.

On walls, tables and shelves, I noticed innumerable strings of beads made of metal, stone, glass, wood, and mother-of-pearl.

"Are these rosaries or prayer-beads?" I asked.

"We have brought together a collection of rosaries from all over the world. Everywhere they are the symbol and instrument of concentration, tranquility, eternal repetition and unity".

"So you hold a kind of religious service here?"

"If you want to call it that—we have not yet found any words which describe what our task actually is. Here, we are neither physicians nor priests; talking to you, one might call us dancers, and therefore artists, for dance and movement are indeed at the root of the arts. We offer a home to our guests in which they can reflect upon their soul, or, as the Germans say, their *Gemüt*. There are so many misconceptions in the world and here they can be forgotten."

Through an arched doorway at one side, I could see a golden altar from the time of the Incas, the original inhabitants of this country. Apart from the massive ornaments and figures starkly carved, the structure resembled a Catholic or East-Indian altar. Here again, rosaries of amethysts or other kinds of semi-precious stones were lying about on big, round tables made of green, polished stone. "Meditation-rooms" was how the angel described a number of loggias and cabins into which apparently thoughtful multi-millionaires needed to withdraw when they were exhausted from shovelling up the dollars. Wherever we went, images and idols, arranged with a surprising sense of colour and form, emerged from the semi-darkness. Then, by way of an underground passage we arrived at a staircase which led to a kind of cloisters. Through the openings we could see a mountain towering over the tops of dark sycamore trees, its contours resembling those of a sleeping bull. Along the mountain's ridge I counted about a dozen smallish buildings standing in regular distances from one another.

"Over there is an age-old Indian place of worship, a kind of Mount Calvary. You should come here at Easter! You would be amazed at the similarities between the religious festivals of our Indians, which are preserved to this day, and the Christian way of worship."

At the end of the cloisters a staircase led down into a vault, built as an extension of a rock-cave. Here behind a golden lattice I saw a frightening, yet marvellous tableau, in which, as in our Christmas-crèches, figures were standing, lying, and sitting around, wrapped in colourful materials and gold ribbons.

"These are mummified Aztec heroes," said my guiding angel softly. "They never knew any other laws but those handed down by custom. They had no kings or princes and even the legendary Red Indian Chief is nothing but a European interpretation of the natural selection of the able, the tribe's heroes, the idolised members of the clan, the priests and healers. The leader of today could serve under his equals tomorrow. The supreme master was the spirit of righteousness which grew from their closeness to Nature. Their fundamental ideas—to keep faith, to have courage, to do one's duty—were mirrored in their way of life and in their arts, as well as in their crafts, buildings and festivals."

"Do you wish then, to initiate as it were, the people who come here into the secrets, or rather into the real substance of the different religions and sciences?"

"We try to compensate as far as possible for the misconceptions which have accumulated through priests and scholars, and for the harm which these have caused. We want to replace doubting and searching with enthusiasm. If priests were to regain the elevated positions they once held," she added pensively, after a short pause, "they would be approximately what we would like to be."

"What kind of music do you really have in the large hall and what else do you do there? Do you have lectures, talks and plays?"

"If you like, I shall be very happy to sing to you later on and introduce you to our music. Language is no barrier to us, but anyone who speaks, sings, dances or lectures here, must be able to sense from the spirit of our community what it is that we need."

"But such people are very rare. They must be quite without conceit and prejudice. It is not at all easy to be ready to be open towards ourselves and towards the wholeness of existence."

"We are free to do or not do what we like, for we bear the responsibility for our doings. Formerly this was taken care of through self-denial in the church or tyranny in the state. We human beings, however, stand between self-denial and authority. Only a god could be wholly servant or wholly master. But don't think that we wish to control our community by anything like discussions or majority decisions. We want to educate our sensitivity towards all that is worth while so that through silent understanding we are safeguarded against hypocrisy."

"But why this style of living which strikes me as awful?"

"We know that in this way we shall come closer to our goal than through poverty which, with the ugliness of need, has no time or strength for higher aspirations. In this sense it is much harder to be rich than poor. The rich often become more easily demoralised than the poor. They grow greedier and emptier, and then come setbacks, illness, degeneration of the family and, in the end, even material impoverishment. From these dangers we want to protect those who have toiled their way up and reached a certain level. We want to give them support and so enable them to use their wealth discerningly."

"I see! So in reality, then, this a school for millionaires?"

"That might be the proper designation for us—school and teachers."

I had always had a great aversion to teachers, but with Miss F. in front of me I could not maintain this.

Miss F. took me back to the hall and asked me to wait there a moment while she would fetch her accompanist and then sing to me. I sat down in one of the armchairs. After a while the manager of the enterprise appeared and asked me if I would care to stay as a guest without any obligation for as long as I liked. A lovely room with a balcony would be put at my disposal, everything would be done to give me the opportunity to get better informed and, if I wanted, to entertain the guests with my art. I asked for time in which to think it over. Suddenly, the organ started up. Never before had music given me such a new experience as these richly resonant sounds, which were answered from the next room by softer tones. Then the angel appeared on the balustrade, dressed in a flowing white gown and sang, some old Red Indian songs. My overcrowded imagination could no longer stand up to this abundance of impressions. I rushed out, collected my friends, pushed them into the car and drove like the devil out into the desert and under the glittering starry sky.

Arizona

For a time, I cruise around in New Mexico and Arizona. I keep thinking how very much this part of the country, its moods, its people and their way of thinking remind me of the land of adventure of my youth. I saw there the same deserts, the same virgin countryside. Both here and there the inhabitants are divided into rulers and ruled. I see the same expressions of hate, the longing for freedom, and the rebellion against alien customs.

In the land of adventure[3] too, the whole population of the occupied provinces was very hostile to us intruders. During my holidays there, we used to gallop in teams of eight up in the thousand-metre-high mountain ranges along the winding roads, our guns at the ready and protected by patrols to the left and right. When a few bullets came whistling past our ears we were not at all surprised. Shooting was the order of the day just as it is here in the West. I remember my father, his adjutant, an orderly and I, on a manoeuvre inspection, riding up a hill from which the whole area could be overlooked, and in the valley opposite us a few companies of our Moslem regiment. I heard the familiar hiss of bullets and saw the sandy soil at our feet burst into tiny clouds.

Down the slope and at full speed we galloped towards the firing unit. A smaller section, having apparently used up all their ammunition, threw away their rifles and tried to escape in all directions behind rocks and shrubs. Soon they were rounded up and taken into custody. Not much of a stir was made over such things.

Strange, too, were the people from a neighbouring country. They possessed ancient cannons which fired huge, round cannonballs of solid iron, things one only finds piled up in arsenals nowadays. It was almost an act of courtesy when they shot a few of these dumplings during the mid-day meal into the barrack yard near the officers' mess just when we were visiting. Once they even hit the roof. We all went outside to inspect it and I shall never forget the picture of the old regimental doctor, who knew little about the customs of the country, standing in amazement in front of the hole. With his napkin tied round his neck in old-fashioned style, he pulled out his pince-nez in order to see the damage better. We laughed heartily but soon had to duck to avoid a second dumpling. These clumsy missiles could be seen flying through the air almost as clearly as birds. The regimental doctor slumped to the ground with shock.

[3] Laban refers back to the time he spent as a youth in Bosnia and Herzegovina, which then belonged to the Austro-Hungarian Empire.

It was not quite so harmless when the people of the neighbouring country viciously caused our patrols to fall down the steep precipices at the frontier. We could never discover how they did it. But several times a month we would find a few of the poor fellows, their necks broken, at the foot of the frontier mountains.

If in one's youth it is considered quite in order to defend oneself if attacked it is really astonishing that people who always live in an ordered bourgeois society make a fuss when there's a bang or hard meets hard. Mostly there is precious little time for sentiments, heroic or otherwise. It was this kind of attitude which I met again in the West. Here, as there, I belong to the enemy-aliens. Why had we come to this country, I asked myself over and over again. In my youth, when I came to the land of adventure as the son of a conquering nation, I was glad to get to know the country, although I was secretly hated and despised. I knew, however, that the people had to hate me, even though they bowed to the ground when I, the pasha's son, as I was called in the land of adventure, rode past on my dapple-grey horse. Yet I felt neither the slightest hatred, nor the least contempt for these people who were so different from me and really only struggled against something unfamiliar. The same is happening here. No wonder that I can follow my curiosity only amid thousands of dangers. However, the little events are unimportant. What is important is the unforgettable dance-experience I take away with me from here.

By chance, I met an old Red Indian who wanted to return to his own kin after a busy life in the "Cities of the Whites," as he put it. He was said to be a hundred years old but looked more like a healthy sixty. He was one of the few Red Indians who, as an entrepreneur in the grand manner, had made a fortune. Though for many decades one of the wealthiest men in the United States, he had never deviated from the customs of his own people in the fundamentals of his way of life. Even in the largest towns he had arranged everything according to Red Indian ways. His meals were prepared by his tribes-

men and no white man was allowed to touch his clothes or
his utensils. When I asked him to tell me something of his
long life he readily agreed. He declared that he considered his life among white people as a sacrifice, and that
he had thought of nothing else but of how to spare his
tribe and, in a wider sense, the members of his race, the
misery which had brought them to the white man's places
of residence and into his service. For this purpose he had
amassed a fortune which he considered the property of
his tribe, and had always arranged to use accordingly.

"Now at last the time has come for me to return to the
bosom of my tribe. Now I shall again have a part in the
soul of my clan, for the individual has no soul, and
without soul we are nothing! Now, I shall go home to die
where I belong."

As he spoke he lifted both his arms up high and from
his wrinkled face his keen eyes gazed steadily into the
distance far above me. Through his kind introductions I
was able to attend a whole series of Indian festivals and
celebrations which a stranger would normally have no
chance of seeing. They were age-old customs and ceremonies in which dance plays a major part. I shall never
forget the laying out of a dead tribal hero. His body was
placed on a buffalo hide, fixed between four thin, swaying poles at a height of about four metres above the
ground. To the accompaniment of chanting the women-
folk, each carrying on their heads an earthenware vessel
filled with gifts, walked from a distant hut some two
hundred metres away in a dead straight line towards the
bier. The file of women divided a large meadow diagon-
ally into two halves. In one half men were driving into the
ground painted totem poles, twice their own size. In the
other half stood an orchestra of drummers which, under
the direction of a dancer armed with a large, feather-
decorated club, continually changed its position. A dance
drama ensued, which consisted mainly of two opposing
parties of approximately one hundred and fifty warriors
in splendid dress each trying to dislodge the others from
their positions with bows and arrows. An incessant rain
of short, wooden, arrows without points poured out

from each side. The warriors, who wore no shields, only avoided the arrows by fantastically agile jumps and turns. As soon as anyone was hit, which did not happen very often, he would withdraw and sit apart. Then one side seemed to gain the upper hand. After half an hour of terrific jumping, and having eliminated about fifty of their opponents, the victorious side, led by the drummers, danced in a long line across to the other half of the meadow. Meanwhile, the women continued walking unswervingly towards the bier. Most remarkable was the achievement of four men who carried a large, heavy tree-trunk through the space. The drummers, frequently dancing and circling, jumped over the tree-trunk without disturbing or missing the precise order of the reverberating beats in the slightest. Then the orchestra became a demon-like, creeping monster, and with muffled frenzied drum rolls incited the dancing warriors into a wild fury.

Having arrived between the poles they began dancing a fertility dance which, as it was explained to me, was addressed to the ancestors and descendants of the departed. The endless evolution of one generation after another was magnificently expressed. New lines of people stormed out from between the chessboard-like totem poles. A few dancers detached themselves from the group and danced particular deeds of the dead man and his ancestors. It was clear that one of them was a skilled scout who moved forwards in all directions, sneaking up, leaping and turning about. Another one was proud and solemn, with commanding gestures. A third stretched out his arms towards the gods; his beseeching gestures caused all the dancers around to stop still for a moment. A fourth stormed through the air with such recklessness that it was almost impossible to follow with the eye his leaps and somersaults. A large circle, within which a fascinating ball game developed, terminated the celebration. Then they danced several times around the swaying bier and eventually disappeared into their tents.

The whole event was led by a singer who ceaselessly muttered narratives and prayer-like invocations. At particular stages of the dance action he broke into gutteral screams and coloratura, while dancing the same movement motif with precision and clarity over and over again just like an automaton. The singer of the Red Indians is a lay priest who even to this day arranges the festivities for the various events of human life. At weddings, births, youth initiations, deaths, illnesses and other misfortunes, when setting out on the war-path and at victory celebrations, it is always the singer, with his brief but appropriate songs and sayings, and still more with his fantastic movement rhythms, who acts as the conquering and confirming, entreating and regulating miracle worker.

The term "singer" therefore, means something quite different from what it means to us. It signifies a human being who, usually adorned with enormous god-like or animal masks, expresses inspirations and inner experiences in a rhythmically enhanced, mysterious way far beyond the ordinary, whether through words, sounds or dance.

The dances of the American Redskins are nearly always rituals and have nothing to do with the theatre at all. A ritual always exhibits greatly simplified movement forms and is never, or only rarely, aimed at solo performance. I saw many more masked dances, fertility dances, war dances, funeral obsequies and medicine dances and it struck me that the individual leaders only stepped forward from their groups to intensify the inner process in which all shared; they never stood out of the community as soloists.

The basic patterns of human movement are probably never so clearly structured as in the dances of the Red Indians. Therefore, to the casual observer they appear to be very simple, even unvaried and monotonous. Yet, the Indian possesses a high dance culture with definite ethical features. But the demon-like elemental powers which come to light are often completely inhuman. It is as if one senses the impact of natural forces, the inner reflection of the raging tornadoes, thunderstorms and catastrophes which sweep this part of the world. One feels the endlessness of open prairies and deserts, and the ruggedness of the towering rocks and mountains, amongst which these people live. But at the same time one perceives that these natural forces have given the Redskins an inner motivation to be free and proud in their endeavours. The great value attached to courage, sincerity, and to a sense of justice bordering on ruthlessness, shows in all their movements. The yearning songs of some of these tribes pour forth the same unbridled primary instinct as their dances. Yet even their most savage stamping is never quite so stupefying and elemental as that of African peoples. The dances of the Red Indians never lead to frenzy. The postures often remind one of Greek or ancient Egyptian sculpture. The grotesqueness is unsophisticated and not evil in nature. Form and direction in space are especially cultivated, and the groups move along lines which make a decorative groundplan of great clarity and beauty. The dance of the black peoples lacks all symbolic form and therefore all clarity of line. Only the flow of energy is important to them. The passionately wild crescendo and decrescendo of body shaking, so richly varied in rhythmical order, which is characteristic of negro tribes, is never seen with the Red Indians.

San Francisco

It seems that man's talent for dance has developed on the side of the world bordering the Pacific Ocean. In this connection, I am also thinking of Asia and the Pacific Islands. There is nothing in the art of movement more versatile and perfected than the Chinese theatre, though it is forced towards a baroque, even rococo-like stylisation. The art of dance of the Red Indian is, in contrast, simple and almost athletic. There is nothing theatrical about it, and the magic of its movement becomes effective through festivals of worship which today, unfortunately, are beginning to die out.

Looking at it broadly, it seems curious that in Asia
dance has become part of play-acting.
The Asian actor is totally different from our actors.
Our "show" performer is much more of a "sound"
performer. There is little to see—at least of live movement. For the Asian actor on the other hand, visual
display, which naturally includes dance, is much to the
fore. While the Red Indian singer deals mostly with
mythological-philisophical material, the Asian actor
focuses more on the representation of human life. The
historical factor is often more prominent and reminiscences of real historical events are very frequent. These
are, of course, things which have to be taken in by the
intellect and must therefore be communicated by means
of the spoken word. But during and in between
the speech, there is mime, which is pure dance-
characterisation and a language in itself, as is the music
which accompanies most of the play. The clearly
delineated trinity of dance—sound—word, makes it possible to look at dance separately. In consequence in dance
the meaning of individual gestures is known to the
general public and in this way dance is used by some
Asian peoples as a narrative language. It would be most
interesting to explore thoroughly the grammar and
syntax of the Asian movement languages. But is it a
question of movement language at all? Isn't it rather
body positions and attitudes which mean the same as, for
instance, a rune? Are they not characters or letters
represented by the body, or even words and sentences
written by it in space?
When I first tried to visit a Chinese theatre I hesitated
at the entrance. I had been warned about China-town,
the Chinese quarter, and I already had a few lively
experiences behind me. During my search for a Chinese
female dancer who had been widely acclaimed and
whose picture had attracted my attention somewhere, I
came upon a house in Chicago which I was allowed to
enter but which it was not at all easy to get out of again. I
had to climb a rickety wooden staircase several storeys
high and found myself on a landing with many small

doors, when suddenly above, beneath and all around, innumerable little doors opened and out stepped slit-eyed creatures dressed in green. They pressed in on me and my companion from all sides. To our enquiries about the dancer who was supposed to perform there at that time, they declared with regretful smiles that they had never heard of her. With that they tried to push us gently through one of the small doors. When we declined their hospitality, they applied stronger tactics. But handing out a few lusty punches we managed to escape their hold, jumped over the bannisters, and landed half a storey below. This small advantage got us to the front door. Once out in the street we disappeared among the cars which, entirely undirected, dashed hither and thither in wild confusion. On a corner, not far away, we found a taxi with a coloured chaffeur whom we hired to take us home. White taxi drivers refuse on principle to drive into the "coloured quarters." I myself believe that the coloured people with whom we encountered these little adventures, are really quite nice. It is, rather, the general race-hatred and sometimes fear of the ruling whites which drives them to all sorts of more or less cunning or ill-contrived attacks. In any event, nothing serious ever happened to me during my quests for dance. On the contrary, I always got on well with these people, though one had to be a little on one's guard.

So I hesitated on the threshold of the Chinese theatre. Such a din came from within that first of all I enquired at the booking office whether some kind of fight was in progress or what on earth was going on. "Music" said the man with a feline grin, so I went inside. It is a strange experience being the only white man among a thousand pungent yellow people. One cannot immediately enjoy the artistic treat that is offered and it also takes time for the ear to disentangle the noise. The music in a Chinese theatre at first seems nothing but crescendoing or decrescendoing noise, the aim being to increase attentiveness, which it succeeds in doing most effectively. Slowly, one begins to understand what is involved and is surprised at the inner wealth which reveals itself here.

It is a distinctive feature of the Chinese theatre that it gives first place to the inner powers of man. This can only be done through a strong emphasis on the dance element. The impulses of individual characters then become visible and one sees how they stream through the whole of the body. Meaning and sound of words are used as accompaniment only, and indeed could almost be left out altogether. But perhaps the verbal commentary is necessary for those who, unlike myself, understand the Chinese language but not the meaning of movement expression.

Costume sets the character off and also stresses the inner forces which he represents. The setting in a Chinese theatre is more than plain. Banderols fastened to the back of a chair to indicate the place are superfluous if only for the fact that most of the audience cannot read them. Men in western dress, in shirt sleeves, sluggishly change these banderols during the play and otherwise appear on the stage from time to time in order to place a cup of tea in a waiter-like manner or to remove this or that property. However, the most eloquent thing is the movement, which frequently develops into pure dance expression, and it is at these moments that the Chinese theatre has its strongest fascination. When two demons fight without touching one another, with bare hands, without weapons, and always one or two paces apart, one gets a strikingly clear picture of the qualities which lead to victory. Everyone knows that one of the two has to succumb, because his ruses and tricks are baser, less honest, and less convincing, whilst the movements of the other radiate dignity, power and clarity of purpose. It is breathtaking to watch how they fight one another, using inner attitudes as weapons, how nobility, despite all its advantages, and its ever replenished radiancy can overcome cunning only by tough wrestling. It is something almost indescribable in words but uniquely worthy of theatre, for it is not a fight of rattling sabres and clumsy prancing or only wrestling or boxing for show with harmless holds, blows, pushes and punches, but the fundamental spirit of combat, the concentrated inner composure. Only through a genuine attitude can this kind of presentation become effective. Victory, the act of killing are not mimed, and neither is dying imitated in a realistic way. One sees only tensions which have an inner significance; virtues against cowardly cunning which defends itself against uprightness and almost destroys it, until the inwardly more splendid quality, at last victorious, gains form in space through the dance gesture. It is a miracle and it leads us to a new kind of emotional experience which we hardly know. The bulk of the audience is carried away if both characters perform their parts well.

In another play one sees a turnkey who, either through neglect of duty or misplaced compassion, has allowed his prisoner to escape, and now is called to account. He faces his stern judges in a quivering dance which not only reveals fear, but all the faults and failings which have led him to this lapse. One can see that he is bribable and feels that law and order are fundamentally burdensome to him. He cannot pull himself together to adopt a loyal attitude, and being too weak for an honest, straightforward life, has to be condemned.

A dandy, who enters to put the heart of a woman to test, is not only elegant and well-dressed. He is, in fact, the essence of dandyism which we recognise in his way of stepping and playing with his walking-stick. A blasé attitude, which overlays all natural feeling, is visible as well as self-love or vanity. His gestures mirror a fickle instability. Indications of both virtues and vices appear equally fleeting and insignificant in him, and from this inner state he draws his devilish powers of seduction. Stirring up passion through coarse fondling and flattery, as we often see it on our stages, is never in evidence here.

Of course, our good actors also bring all these forces into their performance, but only incidentally. Word and sound are the dominating media for the characterisation of inner forces. With us a good orator or singer does not need to over-exert himself in his acting or his mime; his declamation, his voice, suffice. Anything else would be beneath his dignity, so to speak. But it is different in the

Chinese theatre. Here above all the acting must be
powerful. Forces of the inner life and human attributes
must first of all be distinctly recognisable. This is the
wellspring of drama in the Asian theatre.
The illumination of an otherwise invisible world gives
a transformed comprehension of reality. One does not
have a feeling of witnessing a misleading stylisation of
nature, but one gets the sense of being truly led to the
heart of actual occurrences. One sees with one's own eyes
the ultimate motivations of all actions, and aspirations,
and recognises above all the immense importance of
ethical striving towards those values which we call virtues. Emotions stirred by the Chinese theatre reach, in
my opinion, deeper down into our inner self than the
mere call to intellect and compassion offered by the
European theatre.

Along the Mississipi
They say that the white Americans dance negro
dances, but this is a mistaken idea. In fact, the steps are all
of old-English origin, and were subsequently imitated by
the negro and heightened into a virtuoso-grotesque
style. The negro has a tremendous feeling for rhythm
and an inherited mobility which he has preserved from
the memories, still fresh in his mind, of his ancestor's
daily physical struggles with the forces of nature, and
which he has brought to the northern urban life. I doubt
whether the negro is capable of inventing any dance at
all. If one hopes to find any kind of negro dance culture
here, one is in for a big disappointment. A gift for
dance-invention as well as the higher development of the
other arts and sciences seems to be the privilege of other
races. The negro adopts our dance-inventions just as he
adopts our stand-up collar and top hat, and uses them
grotesquely, remodelled to fit his own feeling. Where
music is concerned he seems to possess an inborn talent,
but only for rhythmic, melodic, unsophisticated expression. The fact that the white race has re-adopted distor-
tions of its own dances only shows the lack of taste of the
robot-age and is not a sign of a complete dearth of

original ideas. In America there are a great many pioneers of modern expressive dance, which is usually called "German dance," and indeed resembles our style of dance very closely.

From time to time, I worked out a few dances with some young men and women who put themselves at my disposal. If the dances came off well I would perform them. But I could not guarantee that I would achieve anything of real artistic merit with new and untrained people.

Now there is a charming mobility about young Americans. If you walk along the beach of one of the larger seaside resorts you see hundreds of people, from children to greybeards, moving elegantly along turning somersaults and cartwheels. What we achieve through laborious training in gymnastics and acrobatics seem inborn in these people. Their well-trained bodies are mostly well proportioned, too. But what is missing is the soul. In spite of all the exuberance and feeling which they like to express with vivacity the individual gives the impression of beautiful factory ware, each piece lacking a soul. Hadn't the old centenarian, the Red Indian, also denied the presence of the soul in the individual and only attributed one to the masses, the tribe, the race? Does this strange continent produce only mass souls, no individual ones? It almost seems like it.

In fact, the young people who put themselves at my disposal in various places could not be stimulated into any kind of individual expressive gesture, whilst they could bring off communal expression with the greatest enthusiasm and in every respect precisely and vividly. I therefore decided to fall back on to my old sword-dance of cadet festival fame for the men's group, and with the women I studied parts of a dance from *The Swinging Temple*.

I was very surprised when a scholarly Red Indian who watched the preliminary exercises for the sword-dance, reported that he had once seen exactly the same dance performed by a Red Indian tribe in New Mexico. Since my arrangement of the dance was based on memory of the sword-dance of the mountain-peasants of my native country it seemed to me a further proof of the correctness of the supposition that, in primitive times, this form of dance was spread over the whole globe. As it happened, a Japanese had also once confirmed to me the fact, now long recognised by the authorities in this field, that an ancient, traditional sword-dance haunts the whole world. Only the weapons differ. Sometimes they are swords, at others sticks, and at yet others clubs or axes. The dances came off very well, so that we could show them with a clear conscience and success.

In general, however, the dance activities of the white people in America are strongly influenced by the different races, though least perhaps by the dance-world of the yellow peoples. The black and the red peoples however, have contributed greatly to the birth of the "girl-dance." Here, on the simplest pathways such as a straight line, a diversity of body movements is performed in the sharply accented style of negro dances, and remnants of Scottish and other European steps are combined and mingled with movement motifs of the Red Indians. A conglomeration of only decorative significance is the result. Add to it a good deal of sensuality, and the spirit of the American Show, the Revue, is complete. No exception should be taken to the use of the word "spirit" in this connection. Without joking or sarcasm, there is a spirit which urges playfulness rather than play. This is surely justifiable as a means of relaxation in the overheated struggle for existence. I have seen wonderful shows which, in their foppishness, were almost profound. One should not forget, however, that modern artistic dance received its first impulse from an American woman and her Greek imitations.[4] Perhaps it was even through her that appreciation of dance was first awakened in the white Americans. Anglo-Saxon-tinged romanticism with its feeling for sweet harmony and beauty is, therefore, almost always a garnish to the modern expressive dances of the Americans.

[4] A reference to Isadora Duncan.

Apart from representational dance based on drama and mythology, a wealth of social dances exists in the countries bordering the Pacific. Not only are they performed at every gathering in the forms mentioned above, but everybody present takes part in them, Red Indian and Polynesian more than the Asian. In Asia, they like to have professionals to perform their social dances for them. The dance always has a fixed form. With its national or regional mode of stepping and moving it is characteristic of a particular tribe, of its whole outlook on life and its attitude to combat and work, play and belief.

Several times I wondered whether I should perhaps accept one of the invitations which the angel repeatedly sent me to spend some time in Paradise. At last I wrote to Miss F. as follows: "I cannot decide on a prolonged stay at your place. You are seekers as we all are. We are aware of the realm of the soul but we do not really know what to do with its treasures, and I believe that millionaires know this least of all.

We as artists, and especially we as dancers, have the task of shining a light into the inner world, each in his own way. But what we achieve must not be exclusively for millionaires. Our achievements belong to everyone."

Thus far my reminiscences from my American diary.

A genuine belief in the power of unity, in an unspoiled core within the human being gave me the inspiration for a dance-play, telling of the strength of the common hope which lies in a common will to achieve something better. This is *The Titan*.[5] To the hollow sounds of a kettle drum, groups arranged themselves for a dance together. The women detached themselves from the heavy chain of the bellicose dancers and performed in a light-winged manner to a woodwind melody a dance which expressed their intrinsic nature. Feminine, maternal, simple grace alternated with bold masculine male leaps; a solemn

[5] *The Titan*, a work for mass movement choir, was first performed at the occasions of the Dancers' Congress in Magdeburg in 1927. The music was composed by Rudolf Wagner-Regeny, who was Laban's musical collaborator for a number of years, touring with him, conducting the orchestra and composing.

homage both to grace and to the nobility of strength. There were hints of *The Swinging Temple* again, and a memory of all the dances in the world which I had witnessed on my travels. The purpose of life, as I understand it, is a care for the human as opposed to the robot; a call to save mankind from dying out in hideous confusion; an image of a festival of the future, a mass of life in which all the celebrants in communion of thought, feeling and action, seek the way to a clear goal, namely to enhance their own inner light.

Is it possible to express all this through movement, through dance? Only if the participants know and believe that dance has ethical life and only when they have become able to let this experience infiltrate their demeanour and their movement drive. People were moved by our play; it appealed to them. Only my well-wishers from the city press felt somewhat uncomfortable. Maybe I have hated too much the decadent man in *The Night* and have loved too much *The Titan* who keeps invisible guard over a fully alive community.

PART THREE

Chapter 1

EVERYDAY LIFE AND FESTIVAL

A DANCEMASTER is at his most useful and essential to the community when it comes to arranging festivals. The extraordinary round of festivities and festival performances through which my life ran deserves a chapter of its own. On the first occasion I was only an assistant but I soon rose to the rank of master.

I shall not mention the thousands of small festivities among ourselves and the many groups of people who invited us to brighten up their gatherings with our art. But it is worth recording the sorts of occasions and places where one can dance. From the cradle to the grave there are remembrance days of all kinds, and I think there are few occasions at which we have not danced.

I specially remember a funeral at which a solemn dance was performed, which had been the last request of the deceased who had been a great friend of the art of dance. This lifted the burial service out of its usual mournful atmosphere, and a few people told me that since then they had looked on death with different eyes.

As well as dances of death and other solemn events, happy occasions too give me many insights into people's desires, their devotion to dance, and their need to dance. Considering that within a year we sometimes danced on as many as a hundred or more occasions the reader will understand if I limit myself here to only a modest selection of my activities as festival organiser. Festival plays are written for special occasions. Their content grows out of a particular event and environment. Once, in a large city, I was asked to organise a pageant for the crafts and trades.[1] It so happened that it had long been a dream of mine to arrange a dancing procession and I had made a number of sketches for it years ago, so now I was able to produce firm proposals straight away.

"Of course you will have to teach the people yourself! We certainly want this pageant, but for the people to dance in it . . . ." With these words and a gesture of doubt the great man entrusted me with the organisation of the procession, and then dismissed me. I had to start from scratch. There was a list of a few guild-officials, an empty office in the former imperial riding-school and the comforting reassurance of the tourist-bureau that it would all come right in time. But we had no time! In a few weeks, the giant snake, seven kilometres long with about ten thousand participants, countless decorated floats, costumes, and bands, was to move through the town, and so far nobody yet had shown any desire to come forward and join the crazy professor from Berlin[2] whose mind was made up to lead the whole procession dancing through the city.

It was easy to win the hearts of the young, and to this day I think with gratitude and feeling of the battalion of laundry-girls and milliners who helped my ideas on to victory. It was more difficult to win over the young gentlemen, who at first declined with dignity to do any vigorous movement, though in the end they were very good at it. But it was really bad with the old gentlemen, who were worn out by political and economic struggles and who in endless meetings arrived at decisions which they painstakingly recorded and then abandoned after all. I ran from guild to guild. Invariably, I was received by a distrustful, grave-faced assembly of as many as a hundred or more grey-haired masters who pronounced my attempt at establishing a connection between their

[1] This was the *Festzug des Handwerkes und der Gewerbe* in Vienna, summer of 1929.

[2] At that time Laban had his Choreographic Institute in Berlin.

crafts and dance to be wicked nonsense. Only when they understood that I did not intend to organise a kind of public hop but a representation of the working movements used in their crafts did they begin to grow more amenable.

I had the most interesting experience in connection with this. There is hardly a trade which in its manual operations does not have a tradition of working movements and also a festive application of them. The metal crafts provided no problem. Forging and hammering have a natural rhythm. I myself had to swing a hammer and learn to forge a horse-shoe in a Styrian, Scottish or Italian way. I learnt that furriers beat pelts in the spring with Spanish canes, heard what a wealth of forgotten songs and sayings the shoemakers, tailors, tanners, bakers and hundreds of other craftsmen have, witnessed strange ways of handling and stepping, and out of all this, with perseverance and imagination, wove the dance fabric of the pageant. The most important thing was to enlighten the guilds, from the masters down to the apprentices about their own traditions and to arouse their enthusiasm for them. In most cases this was completely successful and, even after many years, I had the satisfaction of hearing from one or the other that I had given them more than just a festival and a momentary advertisement. Young men, who have since become masters have told me that because of the pageant they turned to their trades with far more understanding and love, and that for them the revival of old traditions especially helped to make their work pleasanter and lighter. On the other hand I had glimpsed the bottomless misery caused by loss of loyalty to work, and at first I sometimes felt so discouraged and disillusioned that I often wished the whole pageant would go to the devil.

Gradually, the conviction grew in me that it was not entirely pointless to awaken in working people a feeling for their work rhythm. As a certain easing of their difficulties and relaxation of their rigidity became increasingly apparent I ignored all resistance and pressed on undaunted with my work. For this gigantic task would only succeed if I went straight for my target and ignored all the antagonism, derision, even, and malice.

In my mind was the simple but disdained idea of dancing, which was regarded so askance, and I had not only to revive feeling gone rusty but also steer through the high tides of passion which were nourished by the political and economic confusion these poor people had to suffer.[3] Until then, as an artist, I had hardly concerned myself with politics and even less with economic questions, which were not within my professional sphere. All at once I found myself confronted with the intrigues and animosities which were the order of the day between trade and industry and between retailer and manufacturer. Quite apart from narrow-minded disputes over competence, which frequently interfered with my arrangements, professional jealousy and class hatred between representatives of the various trades made agreement almost impossible. According to their social standing and material circumstance they made all sorts of impossible requests, usually with the aim of somehow humiliating their professional rivals. All this was not conducive to producing a festive atmosphere.

To many people I soon became a confidant and adviser on these matters, and sometimes even arbitrator when controversies were too strong—all for the sake of the festival. What I got to know at that time about individual fates, filled me with both compassion and horror. When one had established a more or less personal contact with ten thousand strangers, almost as if by magic, and had to share their joys and sorrows, it was impossible to remain unmoved. As always the magic wand which opened their hearts to me was my art. When at least we were able to absorb ourselves in play and movement I witnessed over and over again their tired eyes lighting up and their distress disappearing, at least temporarily. Worst of all, however, and far more serious than the economic differences, was the raging national chaos which occupied

[3] In the 1920s Austria was economically at a very low ebb and politically confused.

their hearts and minds. I had been to many countries and wherever German was spoken I felt at home.[4] Even if a Bavarian grumbled about a Prussian, or if in the north, east or west strange views were circulating about the opposite point of the compass, nowhere had one so much the feeling of a complete uprooting or the impression of a branch dying away on a huge tree as in this large city. People were un-German, and would have liked to be different.

In that region the doubtful honour of being a Berliner—which, by the way, I never had been—led to many a ludicrous incident. I will recount one which speaks for many of them. At a large meeting to which I had eventually managed to bring the hostile trade-brothers together, the essential organisational questions of the pageant were to be clarified. I had, of course, settled on my plan and I was developing it at great length when suddenly a little Bohemian tailor rose to his feet, and asked in his priceless German why it had been necessary to import from Berlin a foreign professor who, with his Prussian imperiousness, had brought nothing but unrest to the honest native trades. My laborious attempts at conciliation seemed to be failing. There were loud grumblings and catcalls, some of them in support of the little tailor, and a few hot-heads pushed towards the platform with the clear intention of pulling me down. Since I was pretty well master of the dialect of the town, where by the way I had once been briefly at school and in the neighbourhood of which I had been born, I shouted out a few words in the local idiom and asked them to compare my pronounciation with the Slovakian stuttering of the previous speaker and decide for themselves who was of longer standing there. The outburst of laughter which followed my banter eased the tension, and in a few minutes we had reached agreement on the programme.

[4] Laban's mother tongue was Hungarian, and French was his second language. But since his work had developed mainly in German-speaking parts of Europe, the German language provided an immediate link with the people.

In all these struggles factiousness played a great part. The tradesmen and artisans belonged to the most diverse political camps. One guild was right-wing, another left-wing, and even within the guilds themselves there were factions which abused and denigrated each other with all their might and main. When it was all overcome it seemed a fantastic miracle that I had succeeded in bringing these contrary fellows to an understanding at all. There was no trace of this awful jumble of convictions when they followed one another dancing happily and peacefully, united in the celebration of craftsmanship. But we were not there for a long time yet. Already at the time of our endless consultations I and my small staff of assistants[5] had completed the designs for the floats, cars and costumes. When judging the designs, the hideous errors in taste that had infiltrated the once so exemplary craftsmanship in this city became very conspicuous. Again there were endless disputes, and every conceivable kind of stupid trash was proposed to me. A helpless, mawkish pathetic love of kitsch was the order of the day. There was hardly ever an original idea of style in which a creative capacity could be sensed. It was pitiful to see the stubbornness and lack of imagination with which the dullest travesty of a faded philistine splendour was defended. Yet another educational task! But in the end the allusion to work rhythm, work attire and work atmosphere was understood. After a few wild attempts to persuade me to accept a cheap strolling theatre of the middle ages as traditional, forms were at last found which also corresponded with my fundamental ideas.

The worst offenders were the painters, sculptors and architects who were called in as consultants by the guilds. If they were not out to flatter the inartistic taste of their employers, they proposed their own home brew which would have made even the hair of a lunatic stand on end. Expressionism was fashionable and there was no distor-

[5] Laban's main assistant was Fritz Klingenbeck, who later became a well-known theatre director, dramaturgist and playwright in Austria. Also assisting was Lotte Krause, later a leading choreographer and dance teacher in Israel.

tion and destruction in representation that was not used to replace a lost and healthy sense of form. The fundamental idea—dance and its possibilities—was fiercely opposed. Never before and nowhere else did I meet such ignorance concerning my ideas as with these disciples of art. To break their resistance with brusque rejection would have injudiciously drawn down on my head the animosity of a large group of people with whom I had after all to work. I therefore took great pains to convince them and finally managed to win over most of these quarrelsome artists to my plans.

Meanwhile my staff had grown considerably in size. To my two small office rooms were added quite a number of halls and workshops on all floors of the huge baroque building. They were essential, as each of the four hundred different trades which wanted to take part needed one or more decorated floats, and a fair number of the participants had to be suitably dressed. The large riding arenas were turned into rehearsal halls and two thousand five hundred young people came every evening after work to prepare for the dancing pageant. They marched, walked, solemnly processed, practised swings and dance steps, and above all did the dance which has its home in that city—the waltz. The waltz in all its variations and forms, many newly created for the occasion, was a kind of red thread running through the whole festival procession. People who were stiff and out of training were taken out and made more flexible with simple gymnastic exercises. Unmusical ones—not many in that city—were "rhythmicised" until they could keep in time with the others. As far as possible I tried not to turn down anyone who wanted to have an active share in our festivity. In one of the halls a hundred girl umbrella-makers rehearsed with their little round sun defences. Charming parasol plays were created and the girls, who were mostly pretty and graceful, were thrilled with them. The milliners and dressmakers paraded in another hall; they were one of the largest groups, several hundred strong. When I wanted to encourage them with praise and said—most rashly—"Excellent, beautiful, made for kissing!" they took me at my word and a few hundred of them lined up for a kiss. It was lovely but rather exhausting.

Every day was full of amusing or serious episodes, liveliness, gaiety and enthusiasm and also of heavy responsibility. By the time the festival came we had all become such bosom friends that I forgot the earlier ill-feeling and happily got down to the last-minute preparations. I shall never forget that night when I conducted the dress rehearsal in the huge quadrangle of the old royal stables in moonlight and under a brilliant starlit sky. In addition to the two thousand five hundred dancers, a number of amusing special groups were present, consisting mostly of professional dancers and actors. Then there were also the craft groups with their occupational dances. A giant loudspeaker was placed high up in the background. Some three thousand participants assembled in procession order, and their costumes were scrutinised for the last time. Then the loudspeaker bellowed out its songs and dances.[6] The leaders took their places and we were off. All around me—for I stood alone in the middle of the quadrangle—began such stepping, gliding, jumping and turning by these thousands as I never beheld before or since. In those hours the dream of a dancing master became a reality. These groups of happy young people dancing round me in the light of the full moon moved me more than the numerous ovations which I had received on the stage over the years. The complex structure of this festive procession had been exacting work. But the marvellous devotion to dance which my young friends showed was worth all the toil of a lifetime. Their enthusiasm was boundless. It was as if everyone was under the spell of the unifying, inspiring power of the dance. Countless people shook my hand, their eyes shining, and my favourite battalion, the little milliner-girls, almost drowned me with a rain of flowers, which they had arranged for the end. It was an unusual experience being buried neck-

[6] Sound amplification was in those days still very crude and a great hazard.

deep in flowers with the dark blue, starry sky above and thousands of ghost-like faces radiant with happiness. The best part of all was that we had no spectators—it was our own festival before the festival. Then as morning drew on it became quite cool. For the last time I refreshed my troupe with coffee and cakes in one of the halls. Another two days and the great event would start. Until then everyone had to get a really good sleep to be fit for dancing and marching on the hot pavements in the June sun. For that we would need all our strength.

But there was no sleep for me. My hours of rest had been very few and far between during the past weeks, and for the last two days I had not even thought of sleep. Four hundred floats had to be inspected, some had to be altered, and others even had to be completely redone. With a fleet of ten motor cars I was continually dashing from one end of the city to the other. The floats, which were being decorated in large engine-halls, often stood so close to each other that work on them was hardly possible. Thirty or forty floats were enough to fill a hall to capacity. So we had to visit a dozen halls in distant parts of the town, sometimes even many times over as we had more trouble with the floats than with the dances. Some odd ideas had to be rejected at the last minute. Here materials were missing, there pieces of wood and some-where else props or ornaments had got lost. In one instance, a sketch had disappeared altogether with the result that the float looked such a monstrosity that it could not be accepted. Here a decorator or chief-artist had fallen ill or got drunk in pleasurable anticipation of the festival, there someone had to be rescued from the clutches of his wife who would not let him go on nightshift for such a doubtful undertaking.

In short, even at this late hour, prejudice, grudges and mishaps tried to interfere and hinder things, or silly misunderstandings threatened to play unexpected tricks. There were my pets, the dear loudspeaker-cars which were to accompany the procession at intervals and supply music in addition to about a hundred orchestras stationed along the route. A trial run provided problems

of every kind. In those days we were only at the beginning of mechanical transmission of music. A sudden
wind would blow the sound away and as soon as the
monsters turned a corner off went the music to which one
was supposed to dance. A remedy had to be found
quickly, and find one we did. But the worst thing was that
a raging wind and rain storm broke out on the night
before the festival and transformed all the outdoor
stands and structures into a pitiful state. If it had not
stopped, the pageant would have had to be called off, and
to this day I do not know how I managed to rush from
place to place to put things right again. On top of all this
there were discussions with the municipal authorities
and the police about traffic regulations and street-
cordons. The music sheets had to be distributed to the
hundred conductors and thousands of musicians in the
right order. Gramophone records were specially made.
Teams of organisers and first-aid parties stood by await-
ing our orders. In short, art and administration were
unified in one hellish round dance, with myself all but
alone in the middle of it, for speed and the capacity to
make decisions were rather unpopular in that city. My
attendants and helpers fell by the wayside one after
another. I took the last of them to an all-night café which
we had chosen as our headquarters. There, propped up
against the walls and soaked to the skin, were my
orderlies in a deep sleep. Then my last remaining old
faithful slumped over the nearest marble-topped table in
that café and sank into snores. I gulped down a glühwein
and hurried on to arrange with the broadcasting station
for an announcement of the starting time of the festival
procession.

At last, towards morning, I am alone in my office.
There, the telephone is already rattling away. Everything
is as grey as grey outside, and rain is quietly enjoying
itself drizzling down the window-panes. It's the radio-
station asking: "Is the festival going to take place or not?"
A difficult half-minute of reflection and then I say down
the telephone "We shall dance whatever happens." What
a responsibility, setting a million spectators into motion,
turning a whole bustling city upside down and all for a

leap in the dark! But there is no choice. Feverish activity begins in the courtyard; some of the floats which were delivered only during the night, are knocked and hammered into shape. I go off to inspect the routes and main stands. It has stopped raining. Organised by two old generals a district has filled up with cars and people. The sun is coming out, it's getting warm, hot, wonderful! At last, the giant snake begins to move and its march-past lasts for hours. From my central stand I direct operations with powerful steam sirens, telephones, messengers on bicycles, radio and flag-signals. Several times I had to dash along the seven-kilometre route by car to where the procession would disband and back again, as incidents were reported over the telephone. Each time, it was more difficult for my car to get through. The spectators became aware of me through the cheers of my dancers, and when I was recognised the cordons in some places were quite useless. The hundreds of thousands of people lining the route got into motion and I was feted in a way which I had never dreamed of. A victorious general might have been used to such things, but a dancing master . . . .

I had certainly fulfilled my task of giving pleasure. After the procession had disbanded, having eaten practically nothing for more than twenty-four hours, I dashed off to a small wayside inn where a grumpy waiter explained that they did not serve food on Sunday afternoons. At last he relented and brought me a snack. All around merry people were chattering. They were discussing the pageant and also talking about me. They had no idea that I was sitting alone in their midst.

At nightfall, I went out into the country with a large group of friends and assistants. On the hills were still the same terraces from which once, many years ago, I had looked down on to the glittering city and seen it as the "Queen of the Night."

One day, while I was busy with the preparations for the pageant, I got a telegram from my assistant in charge of the movement choir of M.,[7] a large town in the west,

[7] Mannheim.

informing me that intrigues had greatly upset the arrangements for a celebration due to take place shortly. Since I used to supervise most festivals in person wherever they were, especially when my own works were performed, I was often obliged to dash by 'plane from one place to the other to look after things. The procedure was usually like this: we would be commissioned to arrange a celebration or festival for a special occasion. In good time, we would form a choir of young people from all walks of life, who enjoyed movement, and give them first of all a thorough body training. My choric works were written down in dance notation and rehearsed by the movement choir from this, very much as an orchestra would learn and rehearse a musical work from the score. I mention this because it is quite a new way of conveying dance compositions which only became possible after decades of painstaking preliminary studies. Until then no serviceable dance notation and no generally accepted movement concepts had been available, such as the notation and musical concepts in the art of music. After the first rehearsals I would take over the direction myself or at least be present at the final rehearsals.

The telegram mentioned above concerned a celebration in the town where, many years ago, I had held my first post in the theatre as ballet master. This theatre was having a jubilee, and at first it was planned that I should produce a new dance work for the occasion. I suggested, however, that the young people of the town as outsiders should be invited to pay homage to the theatre in the grand style. This proposal was accepted, so I sketched out plans for the festival performance and appointed a capable movement choir leader who had to prepare the young volunteers for dancing.[8] I then returned to my other duties, the heaviest at that moment being the organisation of the pageant. After receiving the telegram I immediately boarded a plane and flew down to M. On

[8] The Mannheim National Theatre celebrated its 150th anniversary in 1929. During Laban's absence Martin Gleisner, one of the foremost developers of Laban's Movement Choir idea, directed proceedings, assisted by Harry and Grete Pierenkaemper. Their Jena, Gera and Frankfurt Movement Choirs formed the core of the 500 performers.

arrival, I learnt that a number of our dancers, apparently belonging to various youth corporations, had been forbidden by their organisations to take part in my festival performances. It was not easy to find replacements in this case. These young people had been trained for months and to fill their places with newcomers would have needed much more time than we had. The tactics of the whole affair were not new to me. To alienate trained people at the last moment is almost the same as depriving a general of his troops just before a battle. I signed on new participants and gave them a talk in which I explained that not only had we a responsibility to our work but also to our celebrations and festivals, and I called the celebration "Everyday Life and Festival." The new recruits cheered me and pledged spontaneously and unanimously that they would see it through and work twice as hard during the short time left. To this day I am thankful to these keen young people for having kept their word.

The play itself was a kind of proclamation which stated and emphasised what the new generation needed and expected from the theatre. It was a homage to the theatre in which its importance was stressed and the desire for good theatre affirmed. Speech Choirs provided a frame for the movement-play.[9] The third act began with an epigram crystallising the idea of the play. It went:

> We mirror
> In play
> Not only
> The past.
> We show
> As play
> Not only
> To-day.
> We ask for
> The fruit
> We consider
> The morrow.

[9] Martin Gleisner, who was an actor before he came to Laban, had written the extensive text for the Speech Choirs and studied it with them. He himself took the role of the solo-speaker.

Another epigram accompanied the solemn finale:

> Partnership
> In freedom,
> In gladness
> For all
> . . .
> Solemnly
> Striding
> Together
> In chorus.
> Ever
> Stronger
> Binds
> Mutual
> Love
> Kin
> Town
> Country
> And mankind.
> . . .

The weather was not very special. Half-way through the play, which was held in the stadium, there were short showers of rain, but the many thousands of spectators stayed in their places and followed the show enthusiastically. Not so the press belonging to the factions who wanted to prevent the performance. But their undignified squabbling could not hinder the further development of the movement-choir idea.

I have already mentioned that a large movement-choir took part in this festival procession. When, more than a dozen years ago, a number of young people from all walks of life had come to our courses and lectures to refresh themselves through physical exercise and to study the basic elements of the dance-form developed in Germany nobody had ever heard of a movement-choir, and even the concept of it did not exist either here or anywhere else. Gradually, out of our exercises, grew at first modest, and later more extensive plays which not only appealed greatly to the participants but also to the occasional visitor. These plays differed in many ways from the new dances which originated in the circle of our professional dancers. They were really quite different from what had so far been called dance. The movements were simpler and the basic ideas of the plays were not show or stage biased. We conquered space in common swinging and leaping, in measured, slow stepping or sprightly walking and running. It was soon evident that the interweaving paths as well as the bodily attitudes and kinds of movement accompanying them had an import whose significance is rooted in the human psyche. Audiences were excluded for the time being, except for the occasional chance visitor. The sensitivity and spontaneity of expression of the participants were greatly heightened and clarified through moving together in common rhythm. It was a time when the world was filled with vague unrest on the one hand and a forced desire for unlimited amusement on the other. In both these mental attitudes there was a lack of dignity and innocent enjoyment, of healthy delight in physical ability and of natural poise which is implicit in the human form and its simplest movements. The discovery and practice of this ideal bearing in states of collectedness and in vital dynamic movement became the basis of our first movement-choir plays.

We soon got the impression, which was reinforced by our occasional audiences, that we should show our compositions to the public, for nearly everyone who watched us was stimulated into joining in. Meanwhile, our plays had developed into small choir-works. One of the first was *Dawning Light*,[10] in which we experienced the change from stepping in subdued sadness to the awakening of the revitalising capacity which is dormant

[10] An attempt at translating the German title *Lichtwende*, meaning "solstice," the turning-point of the light, and in this movement-choir work the turn is towards the increase of light. *Lichtwende* was performed by the first movement-choir of 80 lay-dancers in Hamburg in 1923, and it contained a section for percussion only, without any dance, which was executed on the stage by the dancers—an entirely new experience for an audience in those days.

in the body. I emphasise "experienced" and not "presented" because at this stage we had no wish to show or convince an audience—although later on, a presentation-style emerged effortlessly and without our doing. We were solely concerned with experiencing in ourselves and in togetherness the increased vigour of the spiritual-emotional-physical forces which are united in dance. Why? Because we were drawn to it, we benefited from it, and we were inspired by it.

Once during one of our social gatherings the question arose of what name we should give our activities. There was no school, and there were no courses at which anything was taught or drummed in. It was decidedly community dance but not professional dance or social dance in the traditional sense. People who came to join us had no wish to become professional dancers. They liked stage dance—as spectators—and had learnt to appreciate it better since they had come to move themselves. Then from somewhere a voice said: "Really, we are a movement-choir." This designation met with unanimous approval, though we had no idea that this newly-coined word would spread so widely in such a short time. In the lightning speed with which the movement-choir idea travelled through Germany and soon abroad as well, it had quite a chequered career. Though the original pure concept was preserved by us and others, movement-choirs got used for all kinds of other purposes, and were even abused. Well-trained groups of people were ideal for walking-on parts in the theatre, for dance groups and other similar things. They could also be used for representing communal experiences and in no time at all movement-choirs were founded for ideological, political, and even scientific purposes, in which the movement experience retreated into the background and gave way to the conscious representation of some ideology or other. Many groups were formed hurriedly and without adequate preliminary training, and they soon brought the original idea of dance-experience into discredit.

By now it has been proved that a movement-choir festival can hold its own before a dance-critical audience. Such a festival, however, should concentrate not so much on the audience's desire for entertainment as on manifesting the joy of moving together. All things have their evolution. It is indisputable that the movement-choir work preceded the art form of choric dance, and it can be assumed that individual choirs will develop further in the direction of festival productions in the future.

Many members of our movement-choir have since formed their own choirs in various large towns in Germany, and some of them have created valuable choric dance works which have won general acclaim. Experience has shown that the decisive factor at public presentations is always the work itself. If suitable dance-works are created for a movement-choir, then there can be nothing against performing them. But the main aim of the movement-choir must always be the shared experience of the joy of moving. Actually, the expression "joy of moving" does not fully describe the fundamental idea. It is to a great extent an inner experience and, above all, a strengthening of the desire for communion. As in all manifestations of communal art, their effects, origins and aims cannot be described in words. Working in a movement-choir can undoubtedly be considered an artistic accomplishment in the same sense as choral singing, communal music-making, the old way of folk-dancing, or choral speaking. The opinion sometimes expressed that only physical training and gymnastic exercise should be the aim is certainly erroneous. Very fruitful combinations result from the relationship between movement-choir work and other communal art forms mentioned above. As in all dances, music plays an important part, of course, although the movement-choir is one of the dance-forms most easily able to dispense with it. Especially as a group-experience and without an audience, silent dance or movement to percussion accompaniment only will become more and more widespread.

We have now reached a point where the teething troubles of this new art of the people are practically over. Many towns have had movement choirs of some standing for years, and most of them have also been used for performances of choric dance works. There are many

different choric works in existence, and there are also
professional dance-groups in whose distinctive character
one can sense the choric movement experience. The
dance-groups of my best known pupils are excellent
examples of this.[11] We can therefore suppose that the
concept of the movement-choir is no flash in the pan but
with its community-forming elements it will become a
cultural and artistic landmark in a future we all long
for.[12]

Among my dance-works are a number of choric plays
which came into being long before the first movement-
choirs were formed. I am thinking, for instance, of the
open-air festivals on the dance-farm.[13] The nearest in
style to a complete choric play was probably the *Song to the
Sun*, a nature *Reigen* in three parts. On a mountain-
meadow, enclosed by great clumps of trees on its south,
east and north sides, and bordering a steep slope to the
west, we had erected a fire-place of boulders. The
audience sat on three sides against the groups of trees.
On the fourth side, over to the south-west, an opal-
coloured lake[14] was visible far below the slope between

[11] *E.g.* those of Kurt Jooss, Mary Wigman, Dussia Bereska, as well as many
permanent groups at the German theatres.

[12] In the U.K. the movement-choir idea has become widely rooted, naturally
in a different form. The first choir was formed by Lisa Ullmann under the
auspices of the Workers' Educational Association in Plymouth in the
mid-1930s and since the war many movement groups and dance circles
have come into being, and festivals of movement and dance, both for adults
and children, have been conducted. A highlight of these was *Kaleidoscopia
Viva*, a Festival organised by the Laban Art of Movement Guild at the
Albert Hall, London, in 1970. Under the overall direction of Geraldine
Stephenson, one of Laban's pupils and assistants during his later years in
England, fifteen groups contributed to the two-hour performance. Dance
as a means of education is also closely linked with the movement-choir idea
in that it sets out to develop sensibility for movement and dance in everyone
for his own benefit and enjoyment as well as that of the community.

[13] Laban refers here to his work on the Monte Verità in Ascona which
extended over a number of years, not only before World War I but also
during it. The following description is of a festival which took place in the
summer of 1917.

[14] The hills and mountains above Ascona offered an ideal setting for this
dance work, and probably inspired it. Looking in one direction the
enormous expanse of the Lake Maggiore formed the background and in
another, a deep valley spread below with the houses of Locarno clustered in
it.

towering mountains which gradually lost themselves in a range of blue hills. Here we performed the introductory scene of the festive play *Dance of the Setting Sun*. After a solemn *Reigen* round the fire, a speaker, accompanied by attendants, came up the slope. The moment when his head appeared over the edge of the bank was exactly timed so that the lower rim of the setting sun was just touching the horizon. Standing there he spoke the first lines of his poem to the setting sun. Drawing closer and, walking towards the fire, he was encircled by a welcoming group of dancers. He then recited the second passage of the poem, with the sun by now half hidden below the horizon. During the farewell *Reigen* addressed to the sun, women and children came out of the rows of spectators and up to the fire-place to fan the flames. The steeply rising column of thin smoke was wafted this way and that by groups of people continually rushing towards it. Finally there was a poem to the twilight. It was accompanied by a solemn *Reigen* which in the end formed into a procession leading the spectators away from the meadow.

Shortly before midnight began the second part of the play, *Demons of the Night*. A group of dancers with drums, tom-toms and flutes assembled among the spectators, and torches and lanterns lighted up the way to a mountain peak where bizarrely-shaped rocks looked down on a circular meadow. Here five blazing fires were lit and a group of kobolds performed leaping dances around and through them.

Then a group of masked dancers approached. The huge masks, made of twigs and grass, covered their whole bodies. Behind these diverse squatting, towering, angular and spikey shapes hid witches and fiends. Creeping up, they stripped off the disguises of the dancers in a wild scene and burned them. As a finale, around the dying glow of the embers, came the dance of the shadows. Then the torches of the attendants were rekindled and, with dancers in front and behind, the long train of spectators was led back to the starting-point.

These spectators, who had come to us from all over the world, had to go through quite an ordeal. After their night-excursion over hedges and ditches they had to appear at six o'clock in the morning at the third scene of action, on a sloping meadow to the east of the hill. This time, seats were arranged in tiers on the slope, and over the edge below would rise the sun, to which the morning-dance was dedicated. A group of women dressed in loose cloaks of coloured silk rushed up the hill. On the horizon the disc of the rising sun appeared and glowed through the dancers' garments. In a *Reigen* to the awakening day the night spook was dispelled by wave upon wave of people surging onwards, moving joyfully, as a symbol of the ever-returning day-star.

I also remember particularly well the dances for Goethe's *Faust Part II*. In spite of indignant outbursts over my "dance-impudence," audiences had been enthusiastic about them. I produced the most important scenes of the great drama as stylised *Reigen*, framed by those parts of the poetic work which lend themselves to delivery by a speech-choir.[15] The choir was placed out of sight in a raised hemispherical dome. The group dances of the evil spirits, the Walpurgisnight and the finale I count as my most successful compositions.

I set yet another work to accompaniment by speech-choirs. This was *Prometheus*.[16] Here, solo-speakers took the most important roles. The choir sat closely together

[15] This was one of the experiments Laban undertook together with Vilma Mönckeberg-Kollmar in Hamburg at the instigation of the *Deutsche Bühne* in the year 1922. She was "Lektor für Sprechkunst"—lecturer in the art of speech and recitation—at the University, and had collected students, young employees and workmen into a speech-choir. She worked with them on a speech-form arising mainly from the rhythmic-melodic elements of poetry and from the motor activation of the speaker. Laban had transformed the Ernst-Merck-Halle into a three-quarters arena stage on which the movement-choir performed a suite of six choric dances partly in conjunction with the spoken word, partly with musical accompaniment and partly in silence. It was an epoch-making event in the concept of stage production. *Das Hamburger Fremdenblatt* (newspaper) said about it: ". . . the people who had come together to solve the important and highly interesting experiment—word and movement—are competent to pave the way for all those things of which we expect a regeneration in the art of our theatre."

[16] By Aeschylus. The unity of the production was, however, hampered by the professional actors who were engaged for the solo parts. It was said that particularly the male actor, who was a well-known artist from the Hamburg Theatre, was completely "speech-amusical" and "movement-inhibited" in his gestures.

in dark clumps visible to the audience on the right and left of the stage. This ancient work, as is well known, is a fragment. I added as an introduction a dance composition portraying the fetching down of fire from heaven and the chaining of Prometheus to the rock. A huge vulture, danced by three people, threatened the demigod. I also invented and composed a concluding part showing the unbinding of Prometheus through the inner awakening of the people in his care to true cultural values. In the introduction and conclusion no words were spoken; instead I had composed an accompaniment for percussion-instruments which was played by dancers. They were grouped on the staircase leading from the stage into the auditorium and from time to time they crossed the stage in a solemn procession. In an epilogue based on indications in classical writings, I brought the unbinding of Prometheus to a radiant, redeeming close. Our production of this tragedy of a great leader was as successful as the entire festival.

I was very disappointed by a repeat performance of several scenes from these works on the stage of the city theatre. While my dances for *Midsummer-Night's Dream, A Winter's Tale, Faust Part I*, etc., which were composed for the conventional theatrical stage, had been most effective, the massive and sculpturally conceived scenes from *Faust Part II* lost all their appeal for me in the frame of the proscenium arch. Public and press were certainly taken by them but I felt very sad because I saw that a great many of the dance compositions which I visualised needed a specially constructed performance place which could be erected only with great difficulty, and on tours and in other places this would be practically impossible. Later on, for this reason, I did not even attempt to produce my large-scale dance-works in unsuitable places. It narrowed down my repertoire considerably, and as a result many of my favourite works were all too soon forgotten.

My hall in H.,[17] where we performed our first *Reigenwerke* of course bore only a faint resemblance to what I

[17] The Ernst-Merck-Halle in Hamburg.

imagined a dance-space should be. But considering present-day conditions the possibilities were comparatively rich. In this hall I never showed dances with only plastic groupings as I did later in a circus, where the audience could sit all around the stage, but occasionally I arranged for the stage to be extended into the auditorium, so that it was surrounded by seats on three sides.

Actually, the stage in this hall was an ideal large-scale dance-theatre. The only drawback was that it had no tiered seating arrangements, which would have given a complete view of the dance area from every seat. It is obvious that of all the arts dance suffers most from the inability of the audience to see properly. In most halls and many theatres, the dancers' legs are hidden up to the knees by the heads of the people sitting in front. There simply are not any proper dance stages in existence. I have made many sketches and models of suitable places for dance performance, and the first possibility of building one was suggested at the occasion of the World Fair in Chicago.[18] But then the promoters were called away and financial difficulties prevented its construction. One of my favourite projects is a dome, flattened at the top, with the audience sitting in circular tiers of seats. The stage is in the centre of the space and therefore only suitable for plastic dances, which can be looked at from all sides. In this theatre all spectators are approximately at the same distance from the performer. This is very important because in the usual theatre buildings the subtlety of gesture gets lost as the distance from the stage increases while those sitting in front, see details of mime too clearly and at the same time do not have a full view of the whole dance area.[19]

I should like to mention another project of my imagination which is not only intended for large-scale group-performances and pageants but also as a movement

[18] In 1933–4.
[19] A design of a model for a dance theatre is included in this book. (*See also* p. 88.

Fig. 8.—Group sketch for a choric dance-play.

paradise for participants and spectators alike. I call it the "Kilometre-house." An enormous dome would span a stretch of countryside and the whole area would be covered, as if by an artificial vault of heaven, without supporting pillars.[20] I conceived the idea of the kilometre-house in my troubled dreams, when our merciless climate threatened to drown our pageants, open-air-festivals and mass-performances. Having acquired in the course of time a little knowledge of architecture and engineering I do not think the project is impracticable. The dome would be held up by chains stretched as far as possible, in the same way that chain-bridges are suspended. I believe that this idea will be realised sometime in the future when our new ideas of living have found artistic form. Daily free time as well as special festival-times could then give an unexpected impetus to dance-culture.

[20] The conception of such a structure derived from Laban's researches into spatial tensions in movement. It is interesting to see that his vision was much in line with the later experiments of modern architects to create functional spaces in a new way.

Chapter 2

ROADS TO THE FUTURE

APART from choric dance, I was quite definitely aware
that opera dance and an independent highly developed
theatre dance also had to be brought into flower. I
therefore took a path which was only conceivable to me as
a temporary measure and decided to accept guest-
engagements at various theatres as dancer and director
of dance. As I was not in favour of the star system[1] I had
never cast myself as the central figure in my own performances except where absolutely necessary. I served my
art just as wholeheartedly and readily playing small roles
or even pulling the curtain or doing the lights. Whenever
it was important to gain respect for dance of the mature
man I liked to take on this task myself and make a success
of it whether it was a leading part or not. But now I had to
produce works revolving exclusively round myself in the
chief part. I had also to recruit the necessary members of
the cast for each separate occasion, as it proved quite
impossible to support a permanent dance-theatre of my
own from private means. Choric dance is ideal for
festivals and celebrations; but in the theatre and even in
an independent dance-theatre it can represent only one
form among many others. Therefore a repertoire had to

[1] When later on Laban accepted the position of Director of Movement and
Dance at the Prussian State Theatres in 1930–1933 he abolished the star
system at the Berlin State Opera. Besides his belief in involving the whole
group equally in artistic creation, an added reason for this was economy.

165

be composed to meet the requirements of opera and the
dance theatre.[2]

Once again, my thoughts turned back to my childhood.

My uncle, in whose house I grew up, was the city
architect, and in our front hall all the keys of the theatre
were hung up.[3] One of the jobs of the city architect was
to make contracts with visiting companies who came to
our town for longer or shorter seasons. Soon I was
familiar not only with the exterior of the kingdom of the
"faked suns," as I called the flood- and spot-light equip-
ment, but also with the manifold and peculiar pleasures
offered in the theatre. From the flies to the pits there was
no corner which I did not explore. Best of all I liked
opera because it was so colourful and the performers
screamed so beautifully and heart-rendingly.

Strangely, however, I had no desire to become an actor
but I wanted to be a theatre director. I had a curious
conception of a theatre director. Until I was allowed to
watch rehearsals, I thought that he and he alone created
the whole magic: that he painted the scenery, designed
and made the costumes, and told the singers and actors
what to do and say. Then one day I was allowed to attend
a dress rehearsal, and I heard the "almighty" curse and
roar. At his command the stage was dark or light, red,
green or blue. When he shouted: "The moon, the moon,
where is the moon?" a silver sickle rose solemnly into the
midnight-blue sky and when he said: "Too many stars,"
they suddenly went out as if by magic.

By then I already had a notion that God had created
the sun, the moon and the stars. Therefore I concluded
that a theatre director must be something like an aide de

[2] Among Laban's creations at the Berlin State Opera and Kroll Opera were
the *Geisha*, the *Sleeping Beauty*, and many opera dances, for example in
Borodin's *Prince Igor;* J. Strauss' *Night in Venice;* Wagner's *Rienzi,
Tannhäuser* and *Die Meistersinger;* R. Strauss' *Salome;* and Gounod's *Marga-
rete.*

[3] Since Laban's parents were most of the time away from Bratislava during his
boyhood, his uncle Toni (Antoine Sendlein) and aunt Anna, who were very
much the central figures of the large Laban family, took care of him. (*See*
p. 31.)

campe to God. However I noticed to my surprise that my uncle's position was above that of the director. I heard for instance, that my uncle intended to sack him because he did not pay the municipal dues promptly. So the halo with which I had surrounded the head of God's A.D.C. began to fade away, especially when I realised that all he had to do was to shout around and pay dues, while the most beautiful things, such as the costumes and scenery, were made in workshops which I had just discovered. Of the old boy's taste, everyone spoke most disparagingly. But what finally undermined his authority for me was the fact that he did not even write the texts or music himself. According to a remark of the conductor, I learned that the director did not understand anything about the theatre anyway. So I had to consign my first ideal to an early grave.

For a time, I was only allowed rare visits to the theatre, for it was rightly assumed that my imagination would run riot. But I still saw quite a few new things. Earlier on I had already been attracted and moved by Leoncavallo's *Pagliacci*.[4] I now followed with great interest the contest between Puccini and Leoncavallo, who both composed an opera with the same title and content at about that time. This was *La Bohème*.[5] It was the milieu that delighted me as well as everything else.

For some while now, I had chosen to spend all my spare time with my painting master as his apprentice.[6] He had a friend whom I did not like very much but who impressed me with his wild mane and great slouch-hat. He was a journalist and, according to my master, really a poet. While I was occupied with cleaning brushes and setting out paints on the master's palette, jobs which constituted the first part of my training, the journalist-poet used to recite his verses. These two friends as well as others of my master's intimate circle reminded me so

[4] First performed in Milan in 1892.

[5] Puccini's *La Bohème* came out in 1896, so Laban must have seen one of the first performances.

[6] *See* p. 10.

much of the characters in *La Bohème*, that I felt quite at home in this opera.

Operettas and folk-plays which I saw in the open-air arena on the old meadow, had a special appeal to me, for I found the movements so much more amusing and lively than in the straight theatre. I could not make much of my artistic leanings however, because I was already at the grammar school which robbed me of much of my time. How I contrived not to waste too much energy in this useless establishment is still a mystery to me. But I certainly managed to cut down my guest appearances there to a minimum.

In our own narrow circle, I counted as quite a reputable painter. At sixteen, I received prizes and effusive reviews for my pictures at a local art exhibition, and my works adorned the drawing-room walls of my relatives and friends. They were mostly figure-paintings, often peasant scenes in traditional national costumes. My master was an admirer of Defregger.[7]

My theatrical work started in the following way. The old scene-painter died. His son, a friend of mine, applied for his father's job. He was still very young, only a few years my senior. He was excellent at painting rural and architectural scenes, but the human figure always eluded him. This is not necessarily disastrous for a scene painter, but it so happened that after his father's death he was asked to paint a park with a great many statues dotted about in it. In desperation he came to me. I offered to help, and between us we painted on the backcloth fantastic gods, goddesses and centaurs, and water tritons blowing their conch-shells. The scenery turned out beautifully and was generally admired. My friend got his job and as a reward I was allowed to help him with other decors.

Scene painting soon brought me nearer to architecture and so to my uncle's profession. Before long I amused the city buildings department by presenting them with a sketch for a new type of hall which was to be built on the

[7] Franz Defregger, 1835–1921, Tirolean painter.

banks of the great river of my native city.[8] Broad stairs
were to lead to the water, where golden gondolas would
be in readiness. The idea was to have festival productions
on floating stages, while pageants, circuses and suchlike
were to take place in the gardens and in the hall. I
recommended myself as architect, resident-poet and
director all in one go and felt dreadfully snubbed when
my proposals met with roars of laughter.

So I went right over to the performing arts. What I
needed was a variety of practical experience which I tried
to acquire in the most adventurous manner. To the
dismay of my family, I took part in a riding number with
a travelling circus, helped in a conjuring show by project-
ing skeletons on a glass screen and even began to have
instructions from an animal-tamer which almost ended
in tragedy. I had a natural affection for animals and a
great trust in them. This they reciprocated, but animals,
especially large, wild beasts, will not put up with superficial playing about. One must devote oneself to them so to
speak, with one's whole heart, and then in most cases they
are not at all dangerous. Once, when I treated a lion with
an all too easy familiarity, I was saved just in time from
the fury of the great cat by the swiftness of the animal
tamer. My teachers were speechless. But at last they had
the answer to the riddle of why I knew so little about
irregular verbs and such things which were close to their
hearts. "A boy who spends his time with jugglers" ran the
letter addressed to my uncle, "is neither worthy nor
capable of being a pupil of our school." Nevertheless, I
passed my final exams, probably because they were glad
to get rid of me at last.

Soon afterwards, I caused a really unpleasant upset
with an improvised act of stage management. It was the
time when I was just beginning to be chivalrous towards
ladies. It was in the wolves' glen in *Der Freischütz*, when
behind the scenes the shoe-lace of a woman singer, whom
I idolised, came undone. Out in front, on the battle-
field, they were busy wheeling on stuffed fowls, putting

[8] The Danube at Bratislava.

wind-machines in position and rehearsing flashes of lightning. The curtain was due to rise at any minute. Like a perfect gentleman I knelt down in front of my fair lady to fasten her shoelace, when the tenor rushed excitedly into the darkness backstage and tripped up over my elegantly outstretched leg. I suppose he was justified in making biting remarks about loitering louts, but I felt deeply hurt and terribly let down before my lady.

The show piece of the wolves' glen scene was a stuffed wild boar. It would make its appearance under a spotlight just at the most dramatic moment. Like a child's toy it ran on little wheels and was drawn across the stage by a piece of string. The tenor's most brilliant moment was coming. In a flash I reversed the boar, which was in the wings ready for entrance, fastened the string to its other end, and when the cue was given it came joggling across the stage with its quivering little tail first. The effect was indescribable. First the audience began to titter, then there was loud laughter, roars and finally cheers and applause from the gallery. The tenor's aria was ruined. The consequences? I was not allowed to set foot in the theatre any more, which caused a sad break in the development of my theatrical experience and of my only just awakened emotional life.

I am recounting these little adventures because they show how soon I had lost respect for the make-believe-world of the conventional theatre. An excessive rejection of the old-style theatre remained with me for years, until at last, after long searches and struggles, I believed I had found a new approach. But the new ways which were in my mind were not so easy to realise.

The greatest problem was unquestionably the performers. Although during my first engagement in a South German theatre[9] I had rehearsed several works with the resident dance company, for any pieces that demanded particularly expressive movement I had, however, to create a new ensemble. Thus on the one hand there was the difficult task of training a group and on the other I was faced with the rather ticklish problem

[9] Mannheim National Theatre 1921. (*See also* p. 95).

of coming to terms with the theatre and its traditional needs. Up through the trap-door rose a great red pillar on which stood Strömkarl, the nordic god of music. He was supposed to shoot up suddenly to the considerable height of five metres so that with his giant violin he could drive the ever more frenzied Bacclanalia into its final orgies. Something went wrong with the mechanism and I had a long wait before we could continue with the rehearsal. This gave me time to survey the familiar stage operations once again. I had been genuinely keen to accept the offer of a post at this renowned theatre in South Germany, as the possibility of re-creating the dances in some of the operas with my own group and also of giving a ballet-evening on a larger scale attracted me greatly. It seemed to me improbable, however, that the art of dance would reach any great heights here. It was just at that time too that I had my first clashes with the trade unions, whose view of work was utterly opposed to mine. Where my artists and pupils were concerned, I had always wanted to be only the trustee of our common ideals, but the unions caused an unpleasant rift in our work relationship by trying to stamp me as an employer. They not only rejected my requests for a new orientation in all matters of dancers' equity, but they also attacked them with every conceivable weapon, and regarded them with ugly suspicion. Later on, I made short shrift of these people and went my own way until at last, through the dancers' congresses which we called, it became possible to have some influence on the inevitable integration into the state-controlled organisations.[10] In this way we were able to mitigate to some extent the worst damage

[10] At the occasion of the first Dancers' Congress in Magdeburg in 1927, a professional organisation of dancers, who had received a more modern training, was founded and integrated with the Classical Ballet Association under the name *Tänzerbund*—Dancers' Confederation. A Committee under the Chairmanship of Laban was set up to deal with matters such as the artistic problems of the specialist, professional training, plans for a *Tanzhochschule* (recognised college of dance), and copyright questions. The Confederation then became a member of the theatre trade union through which the dancers, dance teachers and movement-choir leaders had representation and gained social security equal to others employed in the theatre.

threatening the arts. But as yet we had no power or task other than to pursue our ideals as best we could and to make them effective through solid artistic work. I would not put up with anything conventional or be lured into cheap superficialities. The power of movement had to speak for itself, and the decor also had to be in tune with it. For years to come I worked in big theatres and did everything possible to instil in them a glimmer of my profound interest in movement. Many renowned directors and theatre managers have assured me that the influence of our example, and especially the dynamism of our group productions has made itself felt in almost every theatre.[11] Numerous theatres have engaged my pupils as choreographers and dancers and many have given the new dance its proper place. All the same, I am of the opinion that the dance theatre of the future will never evolve from the existing theatre.

Strömkarl was the central figure in our new production of the Bacchanalia in Richard Wagner's *Tannhäuser*.[12] Since then, I have become something of a *Tannhäuser* specialist in addition to my many other activities through having been permitted to produce this grandiose vision of the great master in at least a dozen different interpretations in Bayreuth as well as in other leading theatres. At that time I kept to a description which I found in Wagner's writings. It was the original version of a nordic fantasy, and had nothing to do with the classical Roman dance-poem which Wagner later created expressly for Paris. There were no Bacchantes or fauns, no images of Leda and Jupiter or any other figure of the Graeco-Roman world of gods. It was a witches-sabbath with nordic sacrificial rites and with Strömkarl, the demon of music, as the inciter dominating the whole

[11] Egon Vietta, the well-known German dramaturg and writer wrote in 1954: "When in Hamburg after World War I Rudolf von Laban dared to make his first experiments in producing dramas of antiquity in new ways, when he introduced the movement-choir on the stage and revolutionised choreography, this development, although passionately welcomed, was still too early. . . . Nevertheless the breakthrough was made."

[12] In Mannheim in 1921, where Laban had for the first time the chance of producing the *Tannhäuser* Bacchanalia.

scene. In this sketch of Wagner's the passions were not stirred up by beautiful goddesses, but were represented as innate drives. I think I succeeded in realising this concept in my production. One sardonic critic contended, however, that he could not see why the Count and Elisabeth made such a fuss over Tannhäuser "as the latter had not been with Venus but only with Laban." By this he meant that I had eliminated all voluptuousness and mawkish sensuality, and he considered this as a failure on our part to enjoy sensual pleasures. For him, and for others also, there was much too much dancing in it with the result that from then onwards *Tannhäuser* was nicknamed *Tanzhäuser* in our honour. Thus our inroad into the theatre could be called a remarkable success. The battle which began at that time is still being fought today. The resistance does not come from the audiences who went along with us, but from the theatre—the directors and managers, the musicians and stage designers, who are completely in love with their old stage-effects. Even though they have taken over many things from our movement-plays they have not yet quite understood that the spirit of the new stage art must be rooted primarily in the movement expression of the performer. Only then do the inner qualities of the characters become apparent in their full strength and beauty; only then do both the horrifying and the lovely stir the emotions and also become the symbol of deeper values.

In Bayreuth[13] I found my views confirmed, and at the same time I was cured of my excessive rejection of a representational scene theatre by the magnificence offered there. In those years, when foolish little men tried to nibble away at the colossal phenomenon of Richard Wagner in the secret hope that they would eventually be able to throw his works onto the scrap heap,

[13] Laban was in charge of the choreography at Bayreuth for the first time in 1930. He worked under Siegfried Wagner's general direction and with Arturo Toscanini as orchestral director. Seventy dancers took part in the *Tannhäuser* Bacchanalia and Kurt Jooss was rehearsal assistant. An entirely new and dynamic element was introduced in the otherwise traditional production. Siegfried Wagner died that summer before the opening of the Festival. The whole production was, however, repeated in 1931.

I used every means in my power to defend the great art of this master. To me, Wagner was not only a renewer and prophet of the arts of poetry and music. Since both through his writings and from the mouths of his personal collaborators I had the good fortune to get to know his tremendous way of thinking in terms of movement, I can say that he was also a decisive influence on the art of movement. The few musical compositions which he wrote directly for dance are almost the only existing German musical works for theatrical dance. Later, I tried to represent Wagnerian characters in dance using his own music and, despite misgivings, which today, frankly, I share, I was greatly applauded. I also benefited in other ways. I learned to appreciate the master's movement drive, and to this insight I owe much of my knowledge and expertise. Siegfried Wagner supported my endeavours in the most touching and sympathetic manner. He told me several times that my work would have been completely in accordance with his father's ideas. Certainly I never discovered dance scenes in any other operas which suited my own sensibility for movement so well as the unfortunately rare dances in Wagner's music-dramas. My activity in Bayreuth under Siegfried Wagner's direction was, therefore, a time of unclouded joy and inspiration. There I found the link with the stage-forms of our day, by which I mean that I found a new way of using the traditional media.

However, it was not only practical understanding and technical knowledge which I learned from the craft of the theatre people.

It helped me to discern clearly that the art of dance consists of three quite different fields of activity. Apart from theatre dance, which either makes its appearance as dance in opera or in independent theatre dance-works, there are two other forms of dance. One is the festive dance for special occasions, when a kind of occasional dance-poem is composed. Its character is determined by the visual impression it has to make, and its movement content usually shows the reason for the occasion. The other form of dance as an independent art I should like to call the *Reigenwerk*. This kind of art is near to the symphony and the oratorio, and is a celebration of the act of dancing itself. Into this category one can also put all the national dances, as well as those compositions created by the free imagination of the dancer, which are distinct from the dramatic and histrionic spirit of the theatre. The essence of the *Reigenwerk* is the significant mirroring of the inner development of a character, and never the story of external events.

The scope of these different kinds of dance in the fields of opera and the theatre in general is little clarified even today. I have endeavoured to bring about the necessary clarification and, needless to say, have encountered conflicts of greater or lesser severity in the process.

It is even impossible to give only extracts of the numerous opera-ballets which I created over the decades. More important than the names of works familiar to all opera-goers is the fact that here in particular I found that kind of resistance which challenged me to grow and accomplish my best. I am happy to say that in spite of this resistance, and thanks to our spade-work, German traditional theatre-ballet has already come much closer to the contemporary concept of dance.

One of my main concerns was finding new contents for the theatre-dance works. Apart from many fairy-tale and fantasy pieces and movement plays of my own invention, I produced new versions of well-known opera ballets which took into account our need to be touched by dance in the depth of our being. I also had several opportunities in opera and operetta productions to develop the dance and movement potential within these art forms to a level which to my mind is essential for the theatre of the future.

Filled with a new vision of the life of a performer, I could only consider the fostering and adapting of the old-style theatre as a sideline. Over and over again I felt the urge to create an independent dance-theatre.

Works originating during this period had a new and distinctive mark. In the characters of a military leader like Agamemnon, a Don Juan, a Savonarola, or in the comic and tragi-comic figures of a jester, a Casanova and other historical and archetypal personages, I saw not so much the victims of fate, but more the embodiments of ethical values and attitudes. My interpretations were rooted in my own experience of dance and in the potentialities of dance-characterisation and, as far as I can judge, audiences understood them well. Characters concerned with the problems and aspirations of our own time embody particular trends of will. Their fate is almost unimportant. Their inmost being is the scene of ethical struggles out of which are born their deeds, and with them, their destinies. In real life, in addition to the resolution of inner conflicts, an important part is obviously played by events which arise more or less logically or by chance from environment and experience. But they only have a determining and decisive influence on lesser natures. The quality of a deed is either great and noble or small and vain, according to the strength or lack of inner conviction and steadfastness.

Today I feel that the reason why the representation in dance of the above-mentioned characters was so attractive and important to me was because it gave me the opportunity, and even compelled me, to disregard the non-essentials of external influences on a person. Thus I could put the chief emphasis on representing the ethical qualities of his inner disposition. When, for instance, Don Juan's pride and scorn for life mingle, and drive him to an eternal quest for an antithetical female, he is fundamentally longing for humility and love. The path he wants to find in order to be and to become is wrong and, in his sullen and obstinate pursuit of it, he does not shrink from brutality and murder. He has no wish to overcome the obstacles confronting him honestly, but thrusts them aside and destroys them. This is his tragedy. It is not his quest that is wrong, but the path he takes.

All this can be very well expressed and represented in dance without having to bring in the complications arising from environment, chance and unimportant events. Take Agamemnon for instance: what is important is the king and leader; he forgets and neglects his own private life in his struggle for law and order. He cuts himself off from the desire for home and love, and for the sake of fighting he renounces everything that leads to the appreciation of purely human and personal ties. The fact that a murderous hand from within his disrupted family strikes him down and brings to an end an ethical nature which has been stretched too far, is almost of no importance. Agamemnon's portrayal in dance will display his personality and qualities in his dealings with his warriors, enemies and prisoners. Other happenings must not obtrude into the foreground, as they would in a spoken drama.

Thus dance-drama arrives at a completely novel dramaturgy, and finally leads to a new perception of life which tells us of the inner path taken by a character. Whether a higher power exists behind all this is not touched upon. Even if a force of destiny were using a hero as a tool to influence or even to shape world events, the impact of this force would still only become visible in the innate and acquired ethical attitude of the hero and in his inner struggle. Merely to witness incidents does not force us to look too deeply into the nature of events. Only the portrayal of the peculiar fusion of spiritual nobility and human passion which sets external happenings in motion compels us to experience that kind of involvement through which we can come nearer to the deeper meaning of existence.

A materialistic mind would see in this a turning away from the world of facts. On the contrary, there is no turning away, no cowardly attempt to put the blame on extraneous higher powers or the forces of destiny. It is a turning to reality, where the meaning of the development of the hero's true being is found, both in his nature and in the experience of his inner struggles.

Dance is an excellent medium for representing inner attitudes and conflicts. Dance movement leads beyond the usual overestimation of the things of the immediate environment. As a rapid turning movement makes the surrounding objects vanish in the whirl, and the dancer with his inner wrestling seems alone in the world as if on an island, so dance-like thinking and feeling brings about a consciousness of one's innermost self. The physical self disappears, together with the surroundings. The fleeting pathway of the dancer is filled with ethical spirit. The trace, the pathway, the movement are the result of struggle, they represent the victory of an endeavour which, gentle and restrained or wild and abandoned, contains the gift of ethical understanding.

To be able to perceive the pathway of a gesture and in its flow the gift of vital tension at first unnoticed, one has to learn how to look, or perhaps be a dancer oneself. But there are some blessed beings who can open everybody's heart to this gift. It is not the head or brain which is addressed, for this is not the task of the arts, and particularly not of dance. Dance does not speak through the intellect to the heart as does the spoken word; it speaks directly to our hearts, and afterwards perhaps also to the brain, to the intellect. Dance is no static picture, no allegory, but vibrant life itself. We need this direct communication to the heart so much; without it we must surely degenerate.

Here I shall let a foreign critic speak. Ingenuous and unprejudiced, he describes the impact of dance better and more simply than it can be done by a more sophisticated approach. Anyone who has followed the development of the art of dance step by step is apt to lose sight of the whole. The critic says[14]:

"Great interest, stimulation, contradiction, applause —those are the constant companions of all new inventions. We must confess that we went to the theatre as unbelievers, and returned convinced. Having been used to hearing excellent ballet-music at ballet performances, we were astounded at first to see a ballet without music. But we soon discovered that the artistic effect was heightened rather than diminished by its absence. Ballet-music usually made the stronger impact and dance was almost only secondary. Now all at once we experienced dance as a form of art in its own right, stimulating our imagination

[14] Summer, 1924, in Zagreb.

in quite a different way from music. The rhythm of an ornament affects our seeing, the rhythm of music our hearing; the rhythm of movement, however, excites our sense of vitality. Through the rhythm of movement our feeling of being alive is stimulated. We were immediately aware of this sensation when we allowed L.'s new dance-poems to affect us. As young children we used to jump about and dance without music, as young people we enjoyed the movement rhythm in dancing even to the worst music played on the most primitive instruments which did nothing but mark the beat. Eventually we no longer heard even this music but felt our heart, together with that of the dancer, controlling the harmonious movements. And that is surely the highest bliss. Music is superfluous. Indeed, even a narrative of the dance-poem is unnecessary. The dance-idea is soon communicated directly to our feeling. In the end we come to realise that dance as the awakener of the sense of vitality can be an art of the greatest significance."

It might be assumed that music, speaking directly to the emotions, could replace or even outbid dance in this respect. But this is not the case. Music certainly awakens in us an emotional response which is akin to that awakened by dance. A certain desire to move also arises when we listen to music, but it is carrried out only in rare moments. It is a "mood" which remains. Dance seen does not only produce a mood but also a certainty. Dance does not only touch the feelings in a general way but it convinces. In an inspired human being who gives and enhances his whole self, including his body, we can observe the struggles arising from the impulses of his will. Dance reveals a person in that condition in which his whole being overcomes the raw material or, at least, battles against it. The philosopher-poet and the musician too are more detached from life; they communicate through sounds or thoughts. The dancer saturates his living self, his human body, with forces otherwise per-ceptible only separately from it and thus when he places his body before us, it appears in a transcended form. Through this form we can see the source, we can see the very reality of another higher world which we otherwise sense only in our conscience.

Dances which reveal the source in its purest form are rarely seen today. Many search for this purity with unrelenting seriousness and shut all doors with this attitude. Gaiety or even crudity can often allow more insight into the depths of the soul than solemn reserve. Eventually, I had a curious programme. In a few months I created a variety of new works which I had on my mind. There were two in particular, in complete contrast to each other. One of them was *The Night*. In spite of doubts, I decided to produce this fantasy of earlier days after modifying it in the light of my present ideas. The other was *The Titan*. While *The Night* still remained a song of hatred against the soulless robot, the machine man, *Titan* was to show the power of community which I saw lying dormant in people. The basic idea of this work was decidedly choric, but at first I produced it with professional dancers. Later, I handed the notated work over to my trusted movement-choir leader in H.,[15] and he gave it a brilliant production for a festival in the circus building there. (The performance was memorable for me because it was one of the first proofs that a full-length work for many participants can be transmitted through notation.) I visualised the spirit of community like a giant, a Titan, who can and will break all fetters, and open up all the springs of humanity.

Apart from these two works there was still my *Don Juan* to Gluck's music which was constantly in demand, and also a festival play, commissioned by a city. It was the *Ballet of the Knights* set to a shorter early work by Beethoven which I extended into a full-length production by using parts of his *Prometheus* music. The three works, *Ballet of the Knights*, *Night* in its new version for dance, and *Titan* were all created at about the same time and, in spite of their totally different character, they have for me a certain unity. In the *Ballet of the Knights* the past

---

[15] Albrecht Knust in Hamburg reproduced the work in the Circus Busch arena in 1928, to celebrate the fifth anniversary of the Movement-Choirs.

is caught, in *The Night* the present of that time, and in *Titan* I saw the promise of the future, which today, after all these years, seems almost in sight. All three works necessitated an enormous apparatus, as much for the music as for the dance, that is for the large groups of dancers and the orchestra.

I created the *Ballet of the Knights* during my stay in the ancient castle of the city which had commissioned it,[16] and Beethoven is said to have written the music to this ballet at the request of the grand master of an order who had once been the lord of that castle. Now in its deserted halls I rehearsed with my dancers. Down below was a very old park with firs and oaks planted centuries ago. Many of the walls were overgrown with moss and ivy. Broad courtyards, narrow cellars, blunt turrets, gloomy wells and dungeons, faded heraldic banners, and strange crumbling statues all told me their story. A wild night of thunderstorms which I experienced in the park with racing shreds of cloud through which the moon appeared and disappeared until the howling winds brewed up an impenetrable blackness gave me the vision of the life of a Knight. Blinding streaks of lightning lit up the rugged outlines of the roof and pinnacles as brightly as daylight. The roar of the thunder recalled the menacing sounds of the opening bars of the Prometheus music. The silvery early morning, with thousands of dew-drops on the crowns of tree-giants and shrubs, transformed the scenery into a magic garden of diamonds. This is how pages and knights once experienced the break of day. Peasant maidens passed by and an old witch, telling tales of poltergeists and of a headless knight, came hobbling through the gate. When I walked in the dusky evenings through the long passages hung with cobwebs I would not have been surprised to meet goblins and the knight, carrying his head under his arm. The *Ballet of the Knights*

[16] The reknowned spa Bad Mergentheim in South Germany had built a new Kurhalle—the spa's social centre—and the city fathers invited Laban to undertake the ceremonial opening with his chamber-dance group in the summer of 1927. The grand master, who had lived at the famous castle of Mergentheim, belonged to the Teutonic order.

ended with a whirling train of gruesome and enchanting fairy-tale figures. They were lashed by the black storm-banners of the ghostly knights who, in spite of the crosses of St. John on their breasts, were like heathen huntsmen. But before this there was a hunt and a tournament, a pagan peasant-rebellion, nuns defending the new and sacred belief in transcendental love, pages and country-lasses secretly dancing together, with everyone costumed in black and white on a stage devoid of colour. Memories, the past, no literary works, but ghosts which I saw in the castle grounds, on the pinnacles, in the dungeons or on the meadow near the little stream.

The Night was a complete contrast to this, not only in its content but also on account of its reception by the press and the public. While the *Ballet of the Knights* aroused great delight everywhere, *The Night*, as I recounted before, produced abusive comments from the critics and startled the audience; in fact it was a failure as never before, an absolute flop.

To vacillate between excessive hatred and excessive love is a tragic drive. The generally popular dance-play *Don Juan* speaks of these opposites. I produced *Don Juan* in the original version by Gluck, but with a dance-dramatic content which bore my own stamp. As I have mentioned before, this work, in which I danced the leading role, had already been successfully performed in various places for several years.

The final scene in which *Don Juan* is torn in pieces by the spirits of hell, the demons of his love-hate, was fateful for me too. At last I seemed close to realising my aims. My successful works had come near to my ideal of the future dance-theatre. The re-establishment of a permanent stage-dance company was already under discussion. The circle of my permanent collaborators had again widened. Their livelihood was assured by my long-term contracts for the performances of *Don Juan* and other pieces. After much toil and trouble I had at last succeeded in establishing the idea of the male dancer and the masculine dance-style. Engagements for festivals and celebrations were in view, which augured well for movement-choir work. Then came the day of a performance of *Don Juan* in N.[17]

In order to reinforce the infernal chorus which was to destroy me in the role of *Don Juan* in the final scene, a number of movement-choir people had been brought in. Everything went smoothly during the rehearsal, and the evening performance proceeded without a hitch right up to the last scene. The demons, standing on a raised platform, lifted me high, but instead of letting me sink down in their midst, in inexplicable confusion they tossed me into the air over their upstretched arms and I crashed down head over heels on to the stage from a considerable height. A roar of applause is said to have followed my apparently bold leap. I heard nothing for I was unconscious. I just managed to crawl towards the ghostly apparitions in the background and disappear amid the whirling flames of the demons' bodies. That was the end of the performance and—my last dance.

Next day, I found that my left arm was out of action. The doctor also feared internal injury. I would rather not dwell here on the tale of woe which followed the accident. I covered up my injury as best I could, hoping to recover quickly. But it soon became apparent that there could be no thought of returning to the stage for a long time. Every contract had been made conditional on my appearing personally. My physical state and the loss of expected sources of income destroyed all hopes of continuing with my dance-theatre plans for the time being. For a dancer to lose his mobility is the same as for a painter to lose his eye-sight or a musician to go deaf.

Now, more than ever, the value and blessing of notated dance became really clear to me and I began to devote myself with redoubled zest to consolidating and notating my works.

One of the most pressing challenges with which we are confronted is to invent and notate dance-works of value so that they can be performed anywhere over and over again. Much of the decline in enthusiasm for dance,

[17] Nuremberg.

which at times has flared up so brightly, is due to the fact that one hardly catches sight of the dancer's movement—no matter how powerful and magnificent it is—before it disappears irrevocably into nothingness, unless it is written down in notation like literature and music.

What would we know today of Homer, Shakespeare and Goethe, if their works had not been written down? What do we know of the music of Orpheus, or Pythagoras? Nothing, except that it enchanted animals and human beings. But with the invention of music-notation, music began to blossom, and the works of a Bach, a Beethoven and a Wagner could fortunately be preserved. What do we know of the art of dance in the past? A few pictures and statues give us an inkling of the beauty of the movements. A few notes written in old forms of dance notation which we can barely decipher, inform us about some court dance-steps of the last two centuries. But an effective, serviceable notation, able to render the many faces of dance, has yet to be created and made universally applicable. I have paved the way for this and I shall develop it still further.[18] The dances of a Pavlova have already been buried with her. Must we also lose the works of our present dance-generation?

The task of making dance accessible to everyone at festivals and in festive productions has been taken care of through the growth of movement-choirs: thousands of people can now experience the benefit of the rhythm and flow of dance, not only as spectators but also as active participants in the joy of moving. This is something I sought and stood up for passionately all my life. A whole generation of new dance masters, dancers, choir-leaders and dance-teachers went out into the world. They did not always represent things satisfactorily. But this was due to the corruption of the time, which made some of

[18] From the earliest years of his career Laban was convinced that dance could only gain an equal position among the other arts if it had a notation whose principles were universally applicable. He worked towards this end, and after much research and many experiments he established the basis of his kinetography, which was published in 1928.

them look for more lucrative sources of income from the entertainments industry and so be distracted from the real aim. The fruits of my dreams had shot up almost too much, like mushrooms. No wonder that unfortunately I could scarcely recognise my own child any more.

Three important dance-congresses attended by over a thousand people,[19] gave the young dance-generation an opportunity to survey and consolidate their newly-conquered territory. But often more pots were broken than completed. At last, however, they all realised how much still lay before us in the future, and that in itself was a splendid and valuable recognition, for it contained within it the finest thing that life can give—a challenge.

In trying to meet my challenge I have seen how important it is to notate valuable dance works. Otherwise the ardent inner strivings of decades vanish like a breath of air, depriving the impetuous younger generation of the inspiration which the accomplishments of the great can give even after they have departed. I have therefore attempted to adapt to present-day needs a dance-notation, which has been in existence for centuries though known to few, and which approximately resembles our music notation in its system of symbols. The development of a science of dance and a corresponding literature of dance, and with it, written dance became increasingly urgent. For the encouragement and advancement of these aims an organisation of dance enthusiasts formed themselves into a "German Society

[19] The three Congresses mentioned were: (i) Magdeburg in 1927, with approximately 300 people attending—see also p.43. (ii) Essen, 21st–26th June 1928, with over 1,000 participants. Here the discussions centred on the question of the fundamentals of dance training suitable for dancers in general, and there was a multitude of solo, concert and theatrical dance presentations by individuals and groups from various countries, as well as folk and national dances. (iii) Munich, 20th–25th June 1930, attended by an equally large number. Besides a rich programme of theatre-dance, this Congress included dance for the layman. There was a dance festival in which movement choirs from six towns participated, and another one in which groups of children of all ages were included. The themes of the discussions, beside a debate on the social task and situation of the dancer, were concerned with dance as an art form and with the cultural and educational significance of the layman's dance.

FIG. 9.—Design for a dance theatre.

for Written-Dance."[20] The generous leaders of this organisation proceeded then and there to take our young art under their wings.

While theatrical dance had satisfactorily paved new ways, the independent art of dance, the finest flower of all the enthusiasm for dance, was still without a home of its own, though everywhere young people were getting together to form dance-groups of great promise. New, very noteworthy, works were created. Is the work of a single individual really determining this?

For a fleeting moment the performing artist can be a milestone in the development, and then he is forgotten and his impact has ebbed away. But can the quest for the power of beauty ever cease? Amid the multitude of manifestations does not a spark of what others dreamed and created in the past still live on? The bearer of the torch is of no importance. Therefore, whatever is kindled by the fire I fanned, its sparks will return eternally into the light-sphere of noble grace from which they came. God, out of whose radiant abundance the flame came forth, takes care of that.

Reflections in solitude and my gradual recovery led me to new ways in which I could continue to serve my idea in spite of more limited freedom of movement. But many of my dreams and adventures of the last decade are still too fresh in my memory for me to assess now their deeper significance.

---

[20] This society was founded in 1928, and carried on for four years. As its mouthpiece it produced a quarterly magazine, called *Schrifttanz*, which was published by the Universal Edition, Vienna, under the editorship of Alfred Schlee. The Society stood for the encouragement of written dance, the building up of a dance literature with scores of notated dance works, for research, choreology and choreography. After 1932 publications were continued for a time by the magazine *Der Tanz*.

INDEX

189